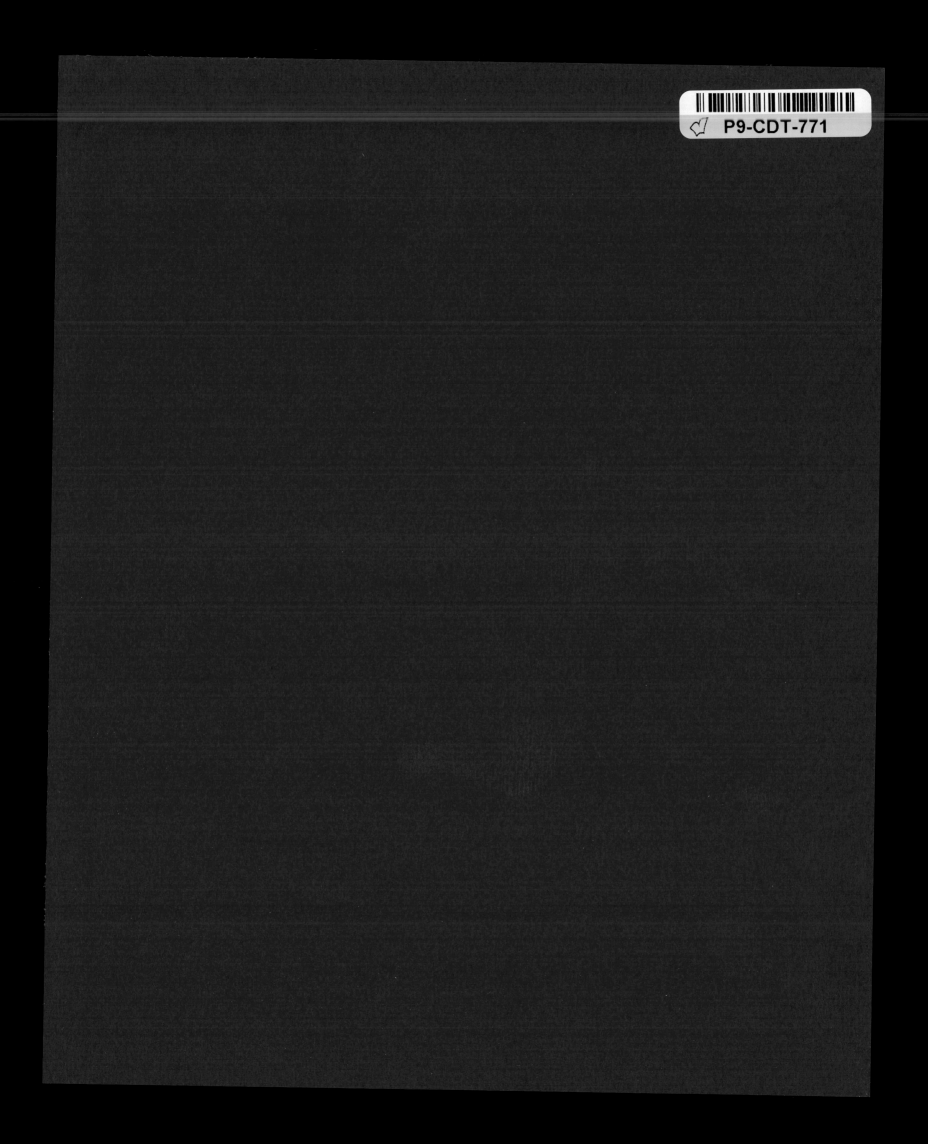

THE BLOODIEST DAY
The Battle of Antietam

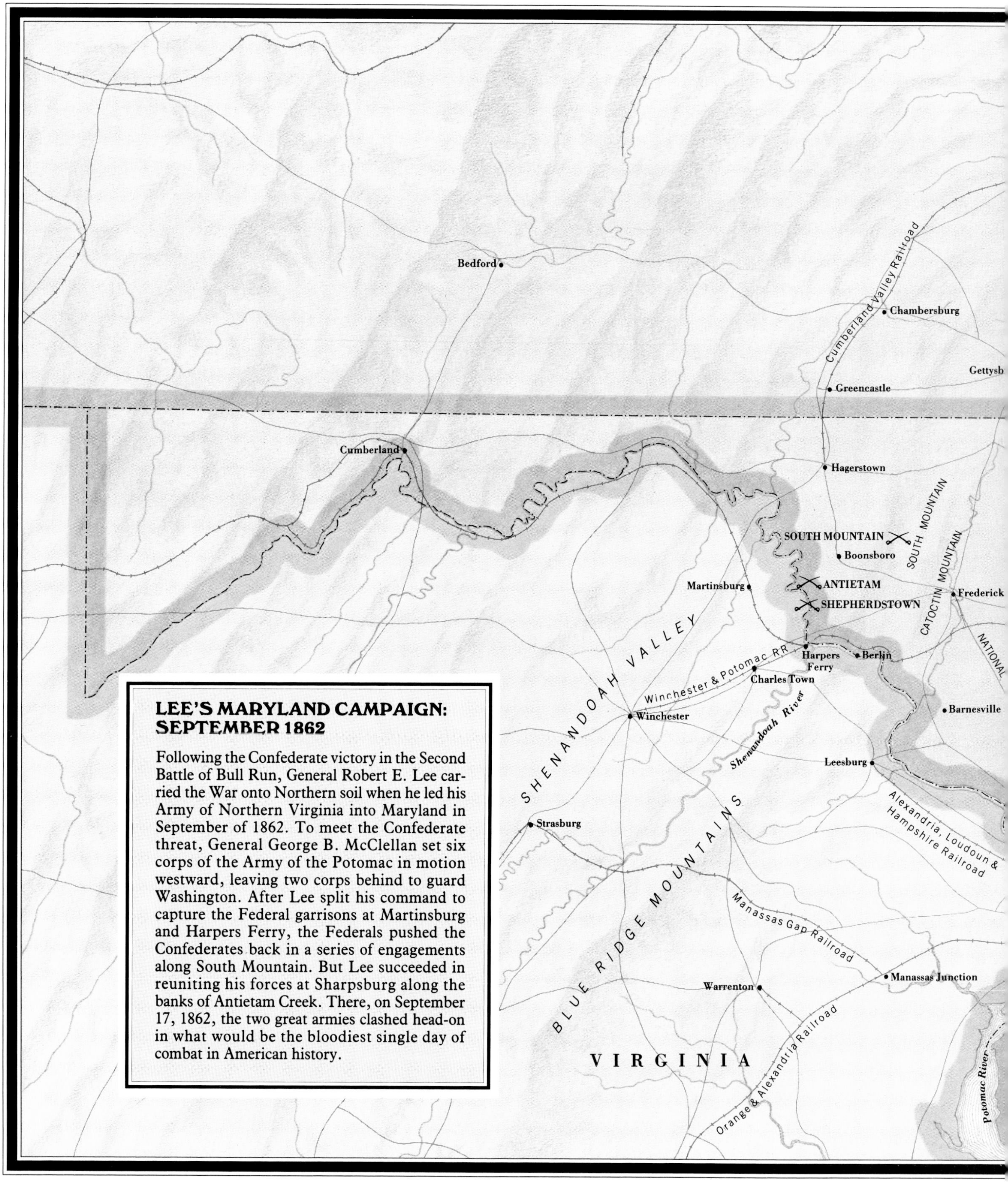

Bedford•

Cumberland Valley Railroad

Chambersburg•

Gettysb

•Greencastle

Cumberland•

•Hagerstown

SOUTH MOUNTAIN ⚔
•Boonsboro

SOUTH MOUNTAIN

CATOCTIN MOUNTAIN

Martinsburg•

⚔ ANTIETAM
⚔ SHEPHERDSTOWN

•Frederick

Winchester & Potomac RR

SHENANDOAH VALLEY

Harpers Ferry
•Berlin

Charles Town

•Barnesville

Shenandoah River

LEE'S MARYLAND CAMPAIGN: SEPTEMBER 1862

Following the Confederate victory in the Second Battle of Bull Run, General Robert E. Lee carried the War onto Northern soil when he led his Army of Northern Virginia into Maryland in September of 1862. To meet the Confederate threat, General George B. McClellan set six corps of the Army of the Potomac in motion westward, leaving two corps behind to guard Washington. After Lee split his command to capture the Federal garrisons at Martinsburg and Harpers Ferry, the Federals pushed the Confederates back in a series of engagements along South Mountain. But Lee succeeded in reuniting his forces at Sharpsburg along the banks of Antietam Creek. There, on September 17, 1862, the two great armies clashed head-on in what would be the bloodiest single day of combat in American history.

•Winchester

Leesburg•

Alexandria, Loudoun & Hampshire Railroad

BLUE RIDGE MOUNTAINS

•Strasburg

Manassas Gap Railroad

Warrenton•

•Manassas Junction

V I R G I N I A

Orange & Alexandria Railroad

Potomac River

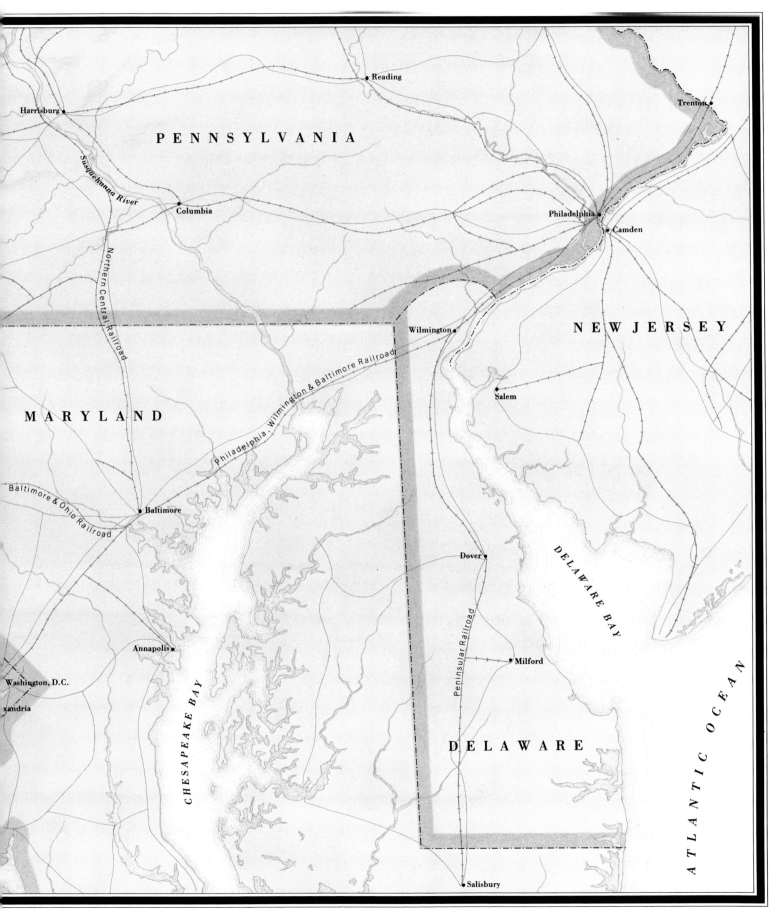

PENNSYLVANIA

Reading

Harrisburg

Susquehanna River

Columbia

Philadelphia

Camden

Trenton

NEW JERSEY

Wilmington

Northern Central Railroad

Philadelphia, Wilmington & Baltimore Railroad

MARYLAND

Salem

Baltimore & Ohio Railroad

Baltimore

Dover

DELAWARE BAY

Annapolis

Peninsular Railroad

Milford

Washington, D.C.

xandria

CHESAPEAKE BAY

DELAWARE

ATLANTIC OCEAN

Salisbury

Scale in Miles

0   25   50   75   100

TIME LIFE BOOKS

Other Publications:

WEIGHT WATCHERS® SMART CHOICE RECIPE COLLECTION
TRUE CRIME
THE AMERICAN INDIANS
THE ART OF WOODWORKING
LOST CIVILIZATIONS
ECHOES OF GLORY
THE NEW FACE OF WAR
HOW THINGS WORK
WINGS OF WAR
CREATIVE EVERYDAY COOKING
COLLECTOR'S LIBRARY OF THE UNKNOWN
CLASSICS OF WORLD WAR II
TIME-LIFE LIBRARY OF CURIOUS AND UNUSUAL FACTS
AMERICAN COUNTRY
VOYAGE THROUGH THE UNIVERSE
THE THIRD REICH
THE TIME-LIFE GARDENER'S GUIDE
MYSTERIES OF THE UNKNOWN
TIME FRAME
FIX IT YOURSELF
FITNESS, HEALTH & NUTRITION
SUCCESSFUL PARENTING
HEALTHY HOME COOKING
UNDERSTANDING COMPUTERS
LIBRARY OF NATIONS
THE ENCHANTED WORLD
THE KODAK LIBRARY OF CREATIVE PHOTOGRAPHY
GREAT MEALS IN MINUTES
PLANET EARTH
COLLECTOR'S LIBRARY OF THE CIVIL WAR
THE EPIC OF FLIGHT
THE GOOD COOK
WORLD WAR II
HOME REPAIR AND IMPROVEMENT
THE OLD WEST

For information on and a full description of any of the Time-Life Books series listed above, please call 1-800-621-7026 or write:
Reader Information
Time-Life Customer Service
P.O. Box C-32068
Richmond, Virginia 23261-2068

This volume is one of a series that chronicles in full the events of the American Civil War, 1861-1865.
Other books in the series include:
Brother against Brother: The War Begins
First Blood: Fort Sumter to Bull Run
The Blockade: Runners and Raiders
The Road to Shiloh: Early Battles in the West
Forward to Richmond: McClellan's Peninsular Campaign
Decoying the Yanks: Jackson's Valley Campaign
Confederate Ordeal: The Southern Home Front
Lee Takes Command: From Seven Days to Second Bull Run
The Coastal War: Chesapeake Bay to Rio Grande
Tenting Tonight: The Soldier's Life
War on the Mississippi: Grant's Vicksburg Campaign
Rebels Resurgent: Fredericksburg to Chancellorsville
Twenty Million Yankees: The Northern Home Front
Gettysburg: The Confederate High Tide
The Struggle for Tennessee: Tupelo to Stones River
The Fight for Chattanooga: Chickamauga to Missionary Ridge
Spies, Scouts and Raiders: Irregular Operations
The Battles for Atlanta: Sherman Moves East
The Killing Ground: Wilderness to Cold Harbor
Sherman's March: Atlanta to the Sea
Death in the Trenches: Grant at Petersburg
War on the Frontier: The Trans-Mississippi West
The Shenandoah in Flames: The Valley Campaign of 1864
Pursuit to Appomattox: The Last Battles
The Assassination: The Death of the President
The Nation Reunited: War's Aftermath
Master Index: An Illustrated Guide

The Cover: Confederate dead lie beside an abandoned limber on the Antietam battlefield east of the Dunker Church. The men were killed during the early-morning fighting on September 17, 1862, as this position was being defended by the Confederate artillery battalion led by Colonel Stephen D. Lee.

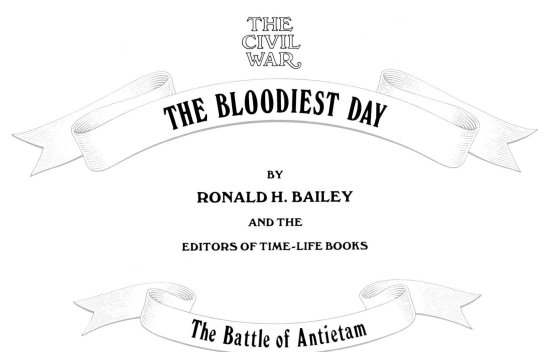

THE CIVIL WAR

THE BLOODIEST DAY

BY

RONALD H. BAILEY

AND THE

EDITORS OF TIME-LIFE BOOKS

The Battle of Antietam

TIME-LIFE BOOKS, ALEXANDRIA, VIRGINIA

TIME-LIFE BOOKS

EDITOR-IN-CHIEF: Thomas H. Flaherty
Director of Editorial Resources: Elise D. Ritter-Clough
Executive Art Director: Ellen Robling
Director of Photography and Research:
John Conrad Weiser
Editorial Board: Dale M. Brown, Janet Cave, Roberta
Conlan, Robert Doyle, Laura Foreman, Jim Hicks,
Rita Thievon Mullin, Henry Woodhead
Assistant Director of Editorial Resources:
Norma E. Shaw

PRESIDENT: John D. Hall

Vice President and Director of Marketing:
Nancy K. Jones
Editorial Director: Russell B. Adams, Jr.
Director of Production Services: Robert N. Carr
Production Manager: Prudence G. Harris
Director of Technology: Eileen Bradley
Supervisor of Quality Control: James King

Editorial Operations
Production: Celia Beattie
Library: Louise D. Forstall
Computer Composition: Deborah G. Tait (Manager),
Monika D. Thayer, Janet Barnes Syring,
Lillian Daniels
Interactive Media Specialist: Patti H. Cass

Time-Life Books is a division of Time Life
Incorporated

PRESIDENT AND CEO: John M. Fahey, Jr.

The Civil War
Series Director: Henry Woodhead
Designer: Herbert H. Quarmby
Chief Researcher: Philip Brandt George

Editorial Staff for *The Bloodiest Day*
Associate Editors: John Newton (text); Jeremy Ross,
Sara Schneidman (pictures)
Staff Writers: Jan Leslie Cook, Allan Fallow,
Glenn McNatt
Researchers: Stephanie Lewis (principal); Harris J.
Andrews, Brian C. Pohanka, Andrea E. Reynolds
Assistant Designers: Cynthia T. Richardson,
Lorraine D. Rivard
Copy Coordinators: Stephen G. Hyslop,
Anthony K. Pordes
Picture Coordinator: Betty H. Weatherley
Editorial Assistant: Audrey Prior Keir
Special Contributor: Paula York-Soderlund

Correspondents: Elisabeth Kraemer-Singh (Bonn);
Margot Hapgood, Dorothy Bacon (London); Miriam
Hsia (New York); Maria Vincenza Aloisi, Josephine du
Brusle (Paris); Ann Natanson (Rome). Valuable
assistance was also provided by: Carolyn Chubet
(New York).

The Author:
Ronald H. Bailey is a freelance journalist and author who
has written on a variety of subjects for Time-Life Books.
He is the author of *Violence and Aggression* in the Human
Behavior series, several volumes in the World War II se-
ries, *Glacier* in the Planet Earth series, and of *Forward to
Richmond* in the Civil War series.

The Consultants:
Colonel John R. Elting, USA (Ret.), a former Associate
Professor at West Point, is the author of *Battles for Scandi-
navia* in the Time-Life Books World War II series and of
*The Battle of Bunker's Hill, The Battles of Saratoga, Mili-
tary History and Atlas of the Napoleonic Wars* and *American
Army Life.* Co-author of *A Dictionary of Soldier Talk,* he is
also editor of the three volumes of *Military Uniforms in
America, 1755-1867,* and associate editor of *The West Point
Atlas of American Wars.*

William A. Frassanito, a Civil War historian and lecturer
specializing in photograph analysis, is the author of two
award-winning studies, *Gettysburg: A Journey in Time* and
*Antietam: The Photographic Legacy of America's Bloodiest
Day,* and a companion volume, *Grant and Lee, The Virginia Campaigns.* He has also served as chief consultant to the
photographic history series *The Image of War.*

Les Jensen, Curator of the U.S. Army Transportation
Museum at Fort Eustis, Virginia, specializes in Civil War
artifacts and is a conservator of historic flags. He is a
contributor to *The Image of War* series, consultant for
numerous Civil War publications and museums, and a
member of the Company of Military Historians. He was
formerly Curator of the Museum of the Confederacy in
Richmond, Virginia.

Michael McAfee specializes in military uniforms and has
been Curator of Uniforms and History at the West Point
Museum since 1970. A fellow of the Company of Military
Historians, he coedited with Colonel Elting *Long Endure:
The Civil War Years,* and he collaborated with Frederick
Todd on *American Military Equipage.* He is the author of
Artillery of the American Revolution, 1775-1783, and has
written numerous articles for *Military Images Magazine.*

Library of Congress Cataloguing in Publication Data
Bailey, Ronald H.
   The bloodiest day.
   (The Civil War)
   Bibliography: p.
   Includes index.
   1. Antietam, Battle of, 1862.
I. Time-Life Books.   II. Title.   III. Series.
E474.65.B3 1984   973.7'33   84-8871
   ISBN 0-8094-4740-1
   ISBN 0-8094-4741-X (lib. bdg.)

CONTENTS

Across the Potomac

"We cannot afford to be idle, and though weaker than our opponents in men and military equipments, must endeavor to harass, if we cannot destroy them."

GENERAL ROBERT E. LEE TO PRESIDENT JEFFERSON DAVIS, SEPTEMBER 3, 1862

1

On Wednesday, September 3, 1862 — four days after his Confederate army's stunning victory at the Second Battle of Bull Run — General Robert E. Lee dispatched a long letter to President Jefferson Davis. The key sentence was the very first one. "The present," Lee wrote, "seems to be the most propitious time since the commencement of the war for the Confederate Army to enter Maryland."

With those words, Lee announced his intention to carry the War onto enemy soil for the first time in the Eastern theater. He would take his Army of Northern Virginia north, into a border state, launching a campaign that would culminate in the fiercest single day of combat in American history and exert a profound influence on the military and political course of the War.

Lee wrote Davis from his headquarters at Chantilly, Virginia, where his troops were resting after the battle there on the 1st of September — a hotly contested coda to the savage fighting around Bull Run. Chantilly was less than 25 miles west of Washington, and the roads leading to the Union's capital were choked with columns of retreating and disheartened Federals. Lee may have been tempted to strike directly at Washington. But even so daring a general knew that such an attack would be foredoomed. The fortifications ringing the capital were too strong. And the Federal armies regrouping there would soon outnumber his Confederates by more than 2 to 1.

Lee had briefly considered two other courses of action. One was to withdraw south behind the Rappahannock River. There he could rest his exhausted army, which as one of Lee's brigadiers phrased it, had been "marching, fighting and starving" since the Seven Days' Battles around Richmond in late June. But this move would allow the Federals time to reorganize and perhaps launch another drive against the Confederate capital.

The other possibility — to remain in northern Virginia — seemed out of the question. Thousands of foraging troops had stripped the fields there of food, and Lee's supply lines were overextended. He lacked the wagons to carry sufficient food for his men and fodder for his horses over the 100-mile route from Richmond.

Moreover, neither alternative would enable the army to sustain its remarkable momentum. Lee wanted to maintain the initiative he had seized outside Richmond.

By invading Maryland, Lee reasoned, he could achieve his immediate military objectives. He could harass the enemy on enemy soil. He could feed his army and horses on Maryland's rich autumn harvest while allowing farmers in northern Virginia to bring in what remained of their crops unmolested by hungry troops. And he could almost certainly lure most of the Federal forces away from Washington, thus preventing another enemy march on Richmond before winter set in.

General Robert E. Lee, portrayed here in an imaginary setting, professed only one fear about his Maryland invasion — running out of ammunition and supplies.

Beyond these military considerations, another set of factors influenced Lee's thinking. He was intrigued by the potential political consequences of entering Maryland. Ever since the Baltimore riots early in the War, there had been signs of pro-Confederate sympathy in Maryland. Many Marylanders were serving in the Southern armies, and as Lee suggested in his letter to Davis, the presence of Confederate troops in the state might afford Maryland "an opportunity of throwing off the oppression to which she is now subject."

Lee also hoped to capitalize on the growing opposition to the War throughout the North. An invasion might strengthen antiwar Democrats in the upcoming November elections and so galvanize discontent that President Abraham Lincoln would be forced to sue for peace.

Furthermore, reports from abroad indicated that Great Britain was greeting with favor the recent Confederate victories. A successful foray into the North might induce the British — and perhaps the French as well — to accord the Confederacy diplomatic recognition and even intervene in the War on its behalf.

Against all the potential benefits, Lee had to weigh one great drawback: the condition of his army. In his letter to Davis, he admitted that "the army is not properly equipped for an invasion of an enemy's territory. It lacks much of the material of war, is feeble in transportation, the animals being much reduced, and the men are poorly provided with clothes, and in thousands of instances are destitute of shoes."

Still, Lee scarcely hesitated. On the morning of September 3, the general broke camp and directed his columns toward the shal-

low fords of the Potomac River just above Leesburg, Virginia, 25 miles to the northwest of Chantilly.

Lee chose this particular destination carefully. It was just east of the Blue Ridge Mountains and only about 30 miles upriver from Washington. The Federals would regard an invasion there as a direct threat to either Washington or Baltimore and would almost surely respond by massing their forces on the north side of the Potomac. This would serve to remove enemy pressure from Lee's supply line through Manassas Junction and give the Confederate troops who had stayed behind time to collect arms and care for the wounded on the battlefields around Bull Run.

Though Lee moved without waiting for approval from President Davis, he was almost certain that his Commander in Chief would sanction the invasion. After all, Lee's mission was merely a foray. He did not intend to occupy enemy territory permanent-

This flag belonged to Company H of the 1st Maryland Infantry, a much-bloodied unit in the Confederate Army of Northern Virginia. Some of Lee's best troops were exiled Marylanders, and he had high hopes that others from the state would flock to the colors once his army was on Maryland soil.

ly, which would have been a sharp departure from Davis' stated policy of fighting only to defend the Southern homeland.

It was a ragtag army that set out for Maryland. The men were gaunt and unshaved, with shaggy hair poking through holes in their shapeless hats. The uniforms of many hung in tatters, held together by bits of rope for belts. Bodies and the shreds that clothed them were filthy and vermin-infested. Only the gleaming rifles were clean.

Thousands of men trudged along in homemade footwear. Still more had no shoes at all.

Maryland women sympathetic to the Confederacy sent this coat of gray English broadcloth through the lines to Robert E. Lee as a gift of welcome. The buttons are decorated with the Maryland state seal.

By one estimate, fully one fourth of Lee's army trod the roads to Leesburg barefoot. Even the new shoes and boots that some had appropriated from the feet of dead Federals at Bull Run were of little use. George S. Bernard of the 12th Virginia tried a pair of boots but found them to be excruciatingly uncomfortable — "as unyielding as if made of cast iron."

Worse than the pain of cut and bruised feet was the gnawing hunger. "For six days not a morsel of bread or meat had gone in our stomachs," noted Private Alexander Hunter of the 17th Virginia. "Our menu consists of apples and corn. We toasted, we burned, we stewed, we boiled, we roasted these two together, and singly, until there was not a man whose form had not caved in, and who had not a bad attack of diarrhea."

Thousands of stragglers, ill and exhausted, fell too far behind to catch up. Others dropped out of the march for reasons of conscience. These men, mostly from the westernmost counties of North and South Carolina, insisted that they had enlisted to defend their homeland, not to invade the North. Still others, natives of northern Virginia, simply got tired of marching and fighting and returned to their nearby homes without benefit of leave, there to sit out the invasion before rejoining their units. So it was that the 8th Virginia, a regiment raised in the region around Leesburg, lost two thirds of its members on the way to the Potomac.

In all, about 15,000 men dropped out of Lee's army during the march. Substantial reinforcements from Richmond did join him along the way — three infantry divisions, a brigade of cavalry and the reserve artillery. But even with these additions, amounting to about 20,000 troops, Lee would enter Maryland with scarcely more than 50,000 men.

To complicate matters, disputes among Lee's generals cost him the services, at least temporarily, of two of the Confederacy's best division commanders. One of them, Brigadier General John Bell Hood, the Kentuckian who had won fame as commander of the Texas Brigade, had been placed under arrest — charged with insubordination in a dispute with Brigadier General Nathan "Shanks" Evans over possession of some captured Federal ambulances. Then, on the morning of September 4, Major General Ambrose Powell Hill ran afoul of his immediate superior, Major General Thomas J. "Stonewall" Jackson. Jackson took careful note that Hill was half an hour late getting his division on the road to Leesburg. Then he

watched with disapproval while Hill rode well ahead of his column, apparently unconcerned by the stream of stragglers trailing off to the rear. Finally, when Hill's column failed to stop for a scheduled rest break, Jackson rode up and angrily halted the lead brigade. Hill came back to find out what was happening, and there was a confrontation.

Furious, Hill unbuckled his sword and offered it to Jackson. Jackson refused the sword but said coldly, "Consider yourself under arrest for neglect of duty." Stripped of his command, Hill then took up a new place — at the rear of his division.

To make matters worse for Lee, he had recently suffered an embarrassing accident. On August 31, the general was standing beside his horse Traveller when a gust of wind blew a map he was reading into the animal's face. Traveller shied; Lee grabbed for the bridle, tripped and fell. Now both of his hands were splinted and bandaged — a bone broken in one, the other severely sprained. Unable to mount his horse, Lee rode instead in an ambulance.

Despite all the problems that beset the Confederates, the astonishing fact was that morale had never been higher. The soldiers who remained were determined veterans. "None but heroes are left," one of them wrote home. In a little more than two months these heroes had driven the Northern invaders from the outskirts of Richmond all the way back to the fortifications around Washington. Now they were about to set foot on Union soil.

On September 4, the vanguard of the army arrived at Leesburg, where the soldiers paused long enough to fill up on food provided by loyal residents and to receive an appropriate benediction from an old woman, who shouted with upraised arms and tearful eyes, "The Lord bless your dirty ragged souls!" That afternoon, Major General Daniel Harvey Hill's division — newly arrived from Richmond — marched on north to the Potomac in advance of Lee's army.

There, without opposition, the invasion of Maryland began. At White's Ford and the other crossing places nearby, the river was half a mile wide, but at this time of year only waist-deep. The Confederates arrived at water's edge in column of fours and halted. They then took off their fraying trousers, slung them over their muskets, shucked off shoes if they had any and, as the bands played "Maryland, My Maryland," waded into the welcome, cool water.

The air was bright and clear, and the setting lovely. Years later the participants could recall in vivid detail their historic moment. "It was a noble spectacle," wrote Major Jedediah Hotchkiss. "The broad river, fringed by lofty trees in full foliage; the exuberant wealth of the autumnal wild flower down to the very margin of the stream and a bright green island stretched away to the right." A cavalryman remembered the sensation of riding onto Maryland's shore: "There were few moments, perhaps, from the beginning to the close of the war, of excitement more intense, of exhiliration more delightful."

The crossing of the narrow ford required the better part of four days, from September 4 through September 7. The only hitch came when a team of balky mules from the wagon train created a traffic jam at midstream. On the Virginia shore, Stonewall Jackson called for his quartermaster, Major John A. Harman, who rode out into the tangle of wagons and let loose a resounding blast of profanity.

Standing on the Maryland shore of the Potomac, a Federal scout takes a pot shot at men of Lee's army as they wade across the river from Virginia at White's Ford on the night of September 4, 1862. When news of the crossing reached Washington, Federal officials were stunned. A member of Lincoln's Cabinet groaned: "The War Department is bewildered, knows but little, does nothing, proposes nothing."

With that, the mules dashed for the Maryland shore. Harmon rode back to Jackson, fully expecting a stern lecture from his pious commander. "The ford is clear, General!" Harmon reported. "There's only one language that will make mules understand on a hot day that they must get out of the water." To the surprise of all, Jackson responded with a grin.

The general then rode out to the middle of the Potomac. There, in a rare dramatic gesture, he doffed his battered old forage cap and posed for all to see. The men let loose with a Rebel yell, and marched on.

In Washington, news of the Confederate crossing hit like an artillery shell. All week, since the Sunday reports of the debacle at Bull Run, something like panic had prevailed among Federal officials. Gunboats had been anchored on the Potomac to defend Washington. The steamer *Wachusett*, according to rumor, stood ready near the Navy Yard to carry President Lincoln and the members of his Cabinet to safety. Companies of hastily organized government clerks took up arms.

One of the first reports of Lee's invasion of Maryland came late on Thursday, September 4, scarcely hours after the Confederate vanguard reached the Potomac. The manner by which the word arrived did nothing to ease the sense of imminent danger: A Maryland farmer on horseback raced like Paul Revere down Pennsylvania Avenue shouting the news. As Lee had intended, the crossing suggested to Federal authorities that the Confederates were about to march on Washington or Baltimore. And meanwhile came news that the Confederate army in Kentucky was massing along the Ohio River across from Cincinnati. Never

Lincoln's reappointment of Major General George B. McClellan as commander of all Federal troops around Washington revived the spirits of officers and men alike. One soldier called the news "almost good enough to cancel the fact that the rebels are now on this side of the river."

had the Union cause seemed so imperiled.

Where hope did exist, it tended to focus on the stocky figure of Major General George B. McClellan. Little Mac, as his troops fondly referred to him, was back in command. Lincoln, just as he had done in July of 1861 after the first Union defeat at Bull Run, had turned to McClellan, naming him on September 2 to command "the fortifications of Washington, and all the troops for the defense of the capital."

To be sure, in the year since McClellan had created the Army of the Potomac, his heroic image had been tarnished by his sluggish Peninsular Campaign, foiled by Lee in the Seven Days' Battles. Even Lincoln had grave doubts. Bringing McClellan back, the President said, was like "curing the bite with the hair of the dog." But, Lincoln told his young secretary, John Hay, "We must use what tools we have. There is no man in the Army who can man these fortifications and lick these troops of ours into shape half as well as he. If he can't fight himself, he excels in making others ready to fight." Lincoln knew that among the top generals in the East, only McClellan had the full confidence of the troops.

Bringing his organizational talents to bear, McClellan merged General John Pope's Army of Virginia into the Army of the Potomac in a matter of days. His restructured command was made up of eight corps. Late on Friday, September 5, McClellan began marching the bulk of his army from Virginia and Washington north and west into Maryland. He would take six of his corps, about 84,000 troops, while leaving two corps behind under Major Generals Samuel Heintzelman and Franz Sigel to defend Washington. The next day, Federal col-

umns thronged the streets of the capital. The lines of march took many of them past the White House. There, that evening, soldiers could be seen resting on the lawn while a tall man in shirt sleeves — the President — moved among them with a dipper and a pail of water.

On Sunday, September 7, the last of Lee's columns crossed the Potomac and caught up with the main body of Confederate troops, encamped around the city of Frederick, about 25 miles northwest of the Federals' new forward base at Rockville.

The reception offered by the citizenry of Frederick was something less than the Confederate soldiers had anticipated. Unlike Baltimore and the communities on Maryland's Eastern Shore, which tended to be proslavery and prosecession, this section of the state contained relatively few sympathizers. The crowds came out, especially the young women, and there was some cheering and waving of Confederate flags. But most of the townspeople appeared to be indifferent; some were hostile to the Confederate cause, and others feared retribution if the Federals returned.

One Union loyalist felt a mixture of contempt, pity and awe as she watched this ragtag band of conquerors march by. "I asked myself in amazement," she wrote to a friend in Baltimore, "were these dirty, lank, ugly specimens of humanity the men that had driven back again and again our splendid legions with their fine discipline, their martial show and colour? I felt humiliated at the thought that this horde of ragamuffins could set our grand army of the Union at defiance. Oh! they are so dirty! I don't think the Potomac River could wash them clean!"

Partly out of compassion, most Mary-

Newly settled into comfortable quarters at a fort outside Washington, First Lieutenant Edward P. Bishop of the 19th Massachusetts enjoys a pipe in a sketch drawn by his tentmate. Exhausted by months of campaigning on the Virginia Peninsula, Bishop and his comrades anticipated a season of restful garrison duty; instead, the unit was ordered into Maryland to pursue Lee's army.

landers treated the troops with kindness, often providing food and water. The soldiers, in turn, behaved themselves. Lee, eager to show the Confederacy's best face, issued strict orders against pillaging. His men were admonished to pay for everything, even the farmers' rail fences they burned to roast their corn.

Lee established his headquarters at Best's Grove, two miles south of town. Under the towering oak trees there, he and his generals received Confederate sympathizers, an awkward task for Lee because his hands were still bandaged and hurting; he chose to dodge the attentions of the young women who rode out in family carriages to see the famous Confederate commander.

Lee's two top subordinates, Stonewall Jackson and Major General James Longstreet, were also suffering from various physical infirmities. Longstreet had a pesky heel blister and limped around headquarters in a carpet slipper. Jackson spent most of the time in his tent resting his painful back, having recently been thrown by a muscular gray mare donated by friendly Marylanders to replace his usual mount, Little Sorrel, which had recently disappeared.

On Sunday night, however, Jackson felt well enough to put in a public appearance. He rode in an ambulance to evening services at Frederick's German Reformed Church. The minister, the Reverend Daniel Zacharias, was a Union man, and despite Jackson's presence, offered up a prayer for the President of the United States. Jackson did not hear it; as was his habit, he had nodded off at the beginning of the sermon.

On the following night, September 8, Lee's cavalry chief, Major General James Ewell Brown (Jeb) Stuart, the most glamorous Confederate of them all, staged a grand ball in a deserted school building at Urbana, several miles southeast of Frederick. Stuart's cavalry was deployed in a 20-mile-long screen, running north-south and centered on Urbana, but there were no Federal patrols in sight. The handsome Stuart, noted one of Jackson's aides, "was ready to see and talk to every good-looking woman."

About 7 p.m., the guests began arriving to find the improvised ballroom festooned with roses and regimental flags. Music was furnished by the band of the 18th Mississippi Infantry, and the hosts were Stuart's officers; before taking to the dance floor they gallantly hung their sabers on the wall. "The strange accompaniments of war added zest to the occasion," wrote Captain William W. Blackford, "and our lovely partners declared that it was perfectly charming."

At the height of the festivities, the lively polkas and quadrilles were interrupted by the distant boom of artillery, then the rattle of small arms. An orderly rushed in to report that a detachment of Federal cavalry had attacked a Confederate outpost, driving in the pickets. Stuart's men buckled on their sabers, called for their horses and clattered off into the night, leaving their startled partners with, in Blackford's words, "every pretty foot rooted to the floor where music had left it."

When Stuart and his officers arrived at the scene of action, they found that troopers from the 1st North Carolina Cavalry already had broken the enemy attack. At about 1 a.m., Stuart and his men returned to the ball to regale their guests with tales of the skirmish.

That same day, in a further effort to garner the good will of the Marylanders, Lee had issued an official proclamation. Addressed "To the People of Maryland," it declared that the army had come prepared "to assist you with the power of its arms in regaining the rights of which you have been despoiled. It is for you to decide your destiny freely and without constraint. This army will respect your choice whatever it may be."

Lee already knew what choice most of the people had made. Many of Frederick's stores had closed, refusing to take Confederate money. Former Maryland Governor Enoch L. Lowe, an ardent Confederate sympathizer thought to wield considerable influence in this part of the state, had not shown up in Frederick despite a telegram from Lee. And while young women might marvel at Stuart and his troopers, no more than 200 Maryland men had joined Lee's army since the invasion. With no citizens' revolt in sight and supplies around Frederick running low, Lee decided that it was time to move on.

It had been in the back of Lee's mind that, if all went well, he might be able to drive as far north as Pennsylvania. From Frederick, he could move his army northwest across Catoctin Mountain and South Mountain to Hagerstown, a distance of about 25 miles. Then, shielded on his right flank by these mountains, he could follow the path of the Cumberland Valley Railroad, which curved 70 miles northeast to Harrisburg, the capital of Pennsylvania. Just west of Harrisburg lay the Susquehanna River and a key bridge of the Pennsylvania Railroad. Destruction of this bridge would sever a vital Federal supply route between East and West. Then, according to Brigadier General John G. Walker, one of Lee's division commanders, Lee said he would turn his attention "to Philadelphia, Baltimore, or Wash-

ington, as may seem best for our interests."

To implement such a plan, Lee would have to safeguard his lines of communication and supply against Federal cavalry raids. This could best be done by shifting those lines westward into the Shenandoah Valley behind the protection afforded by the Blue Ridge. But first Lee would have to deal with two Federal outposts that stood virtually astride his intended supply route in the Valley. At the confluence of the Potomac and Shenandoah Rivers was Harpers Ferry, manned by nearly 12,000 Federals; northwest of that town was a 2,500-man garrison at Martinsburg. Both sites had been isolated by Lee's move into Maryland, and he had assumed they would be evacuated immediately. But the Federal high command, over McClellan's protests, had stubbornly ordered both garrisons to stay put.

To handle this unforeseen circumstance, Lee devised a plan that called for a temporary four-way split of his army. Longstreet, with three divisions, the reserve artillery and the supply trains, would begin the first leg of the movement into Pennsylvania, crossing South Mountain to Boonsboro — halfway to Hagerstown.

Meanwhile, the bulk of the army — six divisions — would eliminate the Federal outposts that threatened the relocation of the Confederate supply lines. In three separate commands, this force would converge upon Harpers Ferry. Jackson, with three divisions, would take a circuitous route west, capturing Martinsburg and then swinging back upon Harpers Ferry. At the same time, two divisions under Major General Lafayette McLaws would descend upon Harpers Ferry from the Maryland side of the Potomac, and General Walker's division would

A column of Confederate troops pauses during their march down a street in Frederick, Maryland, in this rare photograph taken from the second-floor window of J. Rosenstock's store. "They were the dirtiest men I ever saw," a witness noted, "a most ragged, lean and hungry set of wolves. Yet there was a dash about them that the northern men lacked."

The Making of a Union Heroine

When Confederate troops marched through Frederick, Maryland, on September 10, 1862, a myth was born. As the story is told, a child raced into the home of 95-year-old Barbara Frietchie, shouting: "Look out for your flag, the troops are coming!" Thinking the child meant the Federals, the old lady took a small American flag, went out onto her porch and began waving it at the passing soldiers.

Only after several of them told her to go back inside did she realize that the troops were not Federals at all, but the vanguard of Lee's army. Undaunted, she went on waving, despite threats from some of the men. Wishing to avoid an incident, an officer ordered the soldiers on and said: "Go on, Granny, wave your flag as much as you please."

Word of the incident quickly spread, and with each retelling the old lady's act was further embellished and romanticized. Thus enlarged, her deed inspired New England poet John Greenleaf Whittier to set the tale to verse; his composition (below), published in 1863, became a great favorite in the Union.

Southerners were quick to grasp the implications of the poem's popularity. "History is powerless in competition with popular ballad," bemoaned the Richmond *Examiner*. "The uncultivated may pronounce the poem so much nonsense, but the wise know that it will outlive and disprove all histories."

In this fanciful illustration, Stonewall Jackson prevents a soldier from shooting Barbara Frietchie.

Up from the meadows rich with corn,
Clear in the cool September morn,
The clustered spires of Frederick stand
Green-walled by the hills of Maryland.
Round about them orchards sweep,
Apple and peach tree fruited deep,
Fair as a garden of the Lord
To the eyes of the famished rebel horde,
On that pleasant morn of the early fall
When Lee marched over the mountain-wall,
Over the mountains winding down,
Horse and foot, into Frederick town.
Forty flags with their silver stars,
Forty flags with their crimson bars,
Flapped in the morning wind: the sun
Of noon looked down, and saw not one.
Up rose old Barbara Frietchie then,
Bowed with her fourscore years and ten;

Bravest of all in Frederick town,
She took up the flag the men hauled down;
In her attic window the staff she set,
To show that one heart was loyal yet.
Up the street came the rebel tread,
Stonewall Jackson riding ahead.
Under his slouched hat left and right
He glanced; the old flag met his sight.
"Halt!" — the dust-brown ranks stood fast,
"Fire!" — out blazed the rifle blast.
It shivered the window, pane and sash;
It rent the banner with seam and gash.
Quick, as it fell, from the broken staff
Dame Barbara snatched the silken scarf;
She leaned far out on the window-sill,
And shook it forth with a royal will.
"Shoot, if you must, this old gray head,
But spare your country's flag," she said.
A shade of sadness, a blush of shame,
Over the face of the leader came;
The nobler nature within him stirred

To life at that woman's deed and word:
"Who touches a hair on yon gray head
Dies like a dog! March on!" he said.
All day long through Frederick Street
Sounded the tread of marching feet;
All day long that free flag tost
Over the heads of the rebel host.
Ever its torn folds rose and fell
On the loyal winds that loved it well;
And through the hill-gaps sunset light
Shone over it with a warm good-night.
Barbara Frietchie's work is o'er,
And the Rebel rides on his raids no more.
Honor to her! and let a tear
Fall, for her sake, on Stonewall's bier.
Over Barbara Frietchie's grave,
Flag of Freedom and Union, wave!
Peace and order and beauty draw
Round thy symbol of light and law;
And ever the stars above look down
On thy stars below in Frederick town!

recross the Potomac and invest the town from the Virginia side. After reducing the Federal stronghold, all three forces — Jackson's, McLaws' and Walker's — would march north to reunite with Longstreet, ready for further operations.

The entire plan was spelled out in Special Orders No. 191, issued on Tuesday, September 9. Lee's adjutant, Colonel Robert H. Chilton, wrote out copies and had one sent to each of the commanders involved. Since the orders pinpointed Confederate movements over the following few days, several of the recipients took special care to prevent their copies from falling into enemy hands. Longstreet, for example, mentally digested his copy, then chewed it into a pulp.

Jackson, noting that the order detached D. H. Hill's division from his command to follow Longstreet, wanted to make sure that Hill understood that he, Jackson, was aware of the transfer. So Jackson, always careful to maintain security, personally copied the order and sent it to Hill, who read it and put it away for safekeeping. Jackson was unaware that an official copy of Lee's orders had been prepared for Hill. As it happened, that copy never reached its destination. Apparently it got loose and somehow came into the hands of an unidentified Confederate staff officer, who wrapped the document around three fresh cigars and put the package in his pocket.

Early the following morning, Wednesday, September 10, Lee's divided army began to leave Frederick. The soldiers, refreshed after four days of rest, were in a happy mood. They sang along as the regimental bands played "The Girl I Left behind Me," and flirted with young women who came out to watch and wave flags — Union as well as Confederate. A Louisiana artilleryman, William Owen, noticed "a buxom young lady, with laughing black eyes," who had a small Union flag pinned to her dress. "Look h'yar, miss, better take that flag down," one of Owen's comrades yelled out, "We're awful fond of charging breast works." She blushed and smiled, Owen said, "but stuck to her colors."

Jackson, concealing his real objectives, marched his divisions northwestward on the National Road as if heading for Pennsylvania. Jackson even had his officers inquire among the citizens of Frederick for a map of Chambersburg, Pennsylvania. These officers themselves did not know that their goal was Harpers Ferry and that they were now embarked upon Lee's greatest gamble yet.

Lee had defied the maxims of military science before by dividing his army during the Seven Days' Battles and prior to Second Bull Run. But this time he was dividing it into four wings that would be separated by as much as 25 miles for several days. Longstreet had flatly opposed the plan, insisting that the army was "in no condition to divide in the enemy's country."

Lee knew from Jeb Stuart's intelligence reports that the Army of the Potomac was moving out from Washington toward Frederick. But he also was aware from the Northern newspapers that McClellan was back in command, and he was counting on his knowledge of McClellan's temperament. "He is an able general but a very cautious one," General Walker recalled Lee saying. "His army is in a very demoralized and chaotic condition, and will not be prepared for offensive operations — or he will not think it so — for three or four weeks. Before that time I hope to be on the Susquehanna."

Across the Potomac

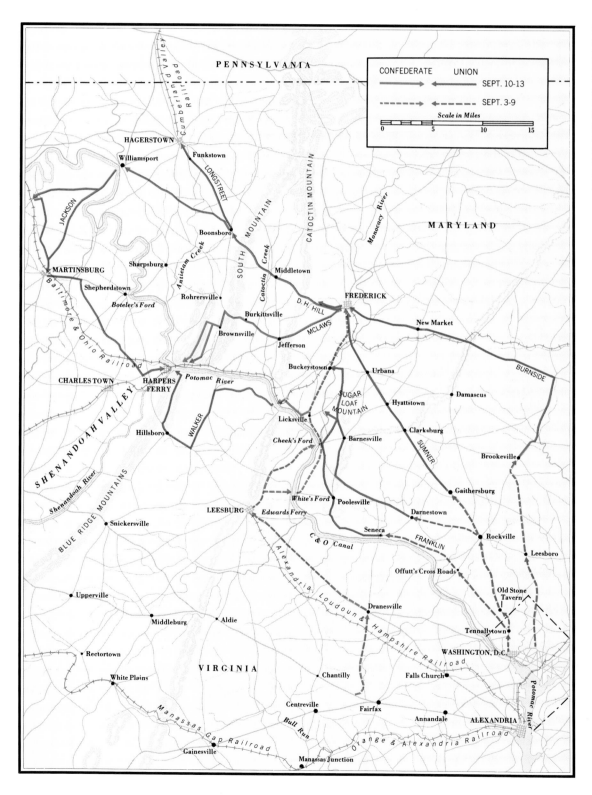

On September 4, 1862, Lee led his army *(red)* across the Potomac near Leesburg and marched into Maryland. At Frederick, he divided his command, sending James Longstreet and D. H. Hill along the National Road toward Hagerstown while Stonewall Jackson, Lafayette McLaws and John Walker attacked Harpers Ferry from three different directions. Meanwhile, the Federals *(blue)* advanced on Frederick in three columns led by Ambrose Burnside, Edwin Sumner and William Franklin.

Lee's assessment was only partially accurate. The Federal army, revitalized under McClellan, was in better physical condition than Lee's. But McClellan was indeed moving cautiously. On September 11, advance elements of the Army of the Potomac were still 15 miles southeast of Frederick. And the army was advancing at an average rate of only six miles a day.

McClellan had good reasons for this deliberate pace. He was uncertain about Lee's intentions; in fact, Jeb Stuart's Confederate horsemen did such an effective job of holding off McClellan's cavalry probes that not until Lee left Frederick was the Union commander certain the Confederate army had been there.

McClellan's caution was reinforced by the entreaties of his superior, General in Chief Henry Halleck. Fretting at his desk in Washington, Halleck feared that Lee's advance into Maryland was only a feint. "It may be the enemy's object," he wired McClellan, "to draw off the mass of our forces and then attempt to attack from the Virginia side of the Potomac."

McClellan was slowed also by the complex reshuffling of his army undertaken on the march. He apportioned his 15 divisions into three wings that proceeded toward Frederick on parallel roads, with the cavalry, under Brigadier General Alfred Pleasonton, in advance. The center wing, under Major General Edwin Sumner, marched along the National Road, which led directly to Frederick. The right wing, under Major General Ambrose Burnside, took a route near the Baltimore & Ohio Railroad. The left wing, under Major General William Franklin, hugged the Maryland shore of the Potomac River. This enabled the army to advance on a 25-mile-wide front that covered the approaches to both Washington and Baltimore. It also provided the necessary concentration in case the Federals had to swing north to meet an invasion of Pennsylvania.

As in his Peninsular Campaign, however, McClellan was hampered by a lack of accurate intelligence about enemy strength. General Pleasonton — misled by exaggerated reports from civilians and prisoners, and by false stories planted by Stuart's troopers — asserted that the Confederates had crossed the Potomac "over 100,000 strong." Other estimates from Allan Pinkerton, McClellan's chief of intelligence, ranged up to 200,000. By the 11th of September, McClellan, who was always ready to believe the worst about enemy numbers, had concluded that the invaders amounted to "not less than 120,000 men" — more than twice Lee's actual strength — and he was asking Washington for reinforcements.

McClellan's leisurely pace toward Frederick suited his soldiers just fine. They were glad to be back on friendly soil after months of campaigning in hostile Virginia. The weather was warm and dry, and the landscape was lovely. The young women who brought the troops bread, fruit and washtubs of lemonade were an added blessing. "It was cheering to see their pleasant faces," Major John M. Gould of the 10th Maine wrote in his diary, recalling the days in "the Virginia wilderness, where the few women have ruined their faces by looking sour."

Less eager to impress the citizenry than were the Confederates, the Federals tended to be freer about living off the land. Lieutenant Thomas Livermore of the 5th New Hampshire recalled a foraging expedition launched when his commander, Colonel Edward E. Cross, spotted a flock of sheep.

"Mr. Livermore," Cross instructed him, "don't you on any account let two of your men go out and get one of those sheep for supper."

"No, sir!" responded Livermore, who promptly ordered two privates to go out and get one sheep each. The two men stalked and ran down the animals and carried them over their shoulders into the cover of a woods. Livermore related: "I sent iron kettles to them, which were soon returned filled with mutton and nicely covered with green leaves. I sent one kettle to the colonel with my compliments, telling him that it contained rations I had drawn. He returned his thanks and caution against leaving any part of them in sight."

Higher commanders adhered more closely to orders McClellan had issued against pillaging. When men of the 23rd Ohio appropriated some straw for bedding, the IX Corps commander, Major General Jesse L. Reno, came thundering up and gave them a verbal thrashing. The 23rd happened to have on its roster two future Presidents of the United States: Lieutenant Colonel Rutherford B. Hayes and Sergeant William McKinley. Hayes was the regimental commander, and he stepped forward to defend the conduct of his men. "Well," he said to Reno after listening to him rant on, "I trust our generals will exhibit the same energy in dealing with our foes that they do in the treatment of their friends." Reno let the remark pass.

As the Army of the Potomac neared Frederick, McClellan stepped up the pace. On Thursday night, September 11, he received reliable reports that Lee had withdrawn from the city. On Friday, he pushed the van-

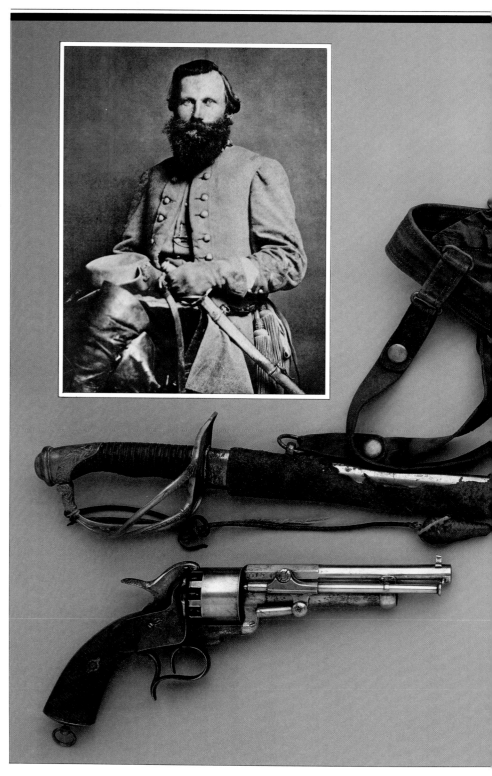

Trappings of a Cavalier

Major General J.E.B. (Jeb) Stuart (*upper left*), Lee's 29-year-old cavalry chief, always fought with a flair. The rakish Virginian wore hip-length boots, a silk sash, bright yellow gloves and a jaunty slouch hat with a black ostrich feather. In addition to a cavalry saber, he carried a nine-shot revolver with a lower barrel that fired a .20-gauge load of buckshot.

guard of Burnside's right wing rapidly toward Frederick.

Lee, in fact, had not completely abandoned the area. He had left a rear guard of cavalry under Brigadier General Wade Hampton to slow the Federals. That Friday afternoon Brigadier General Jacob D. Cox's Kanawha Division ran into part of Hampton's rear guard at the Monocacy River, half a mile east of Frederick. The Confederates were quickly driven back, but one of the Federal brigade commanders, Colonel Augustus Moor, proved to be too impetuous in pursuit. He took a cavalry troop and a single artillery piece and charged headlong into town.

Waiting for Moor at the corner of Market and Patrick Streets were Hampton's troopers. While excited citizens peered out from behind their shuttered windows, the Confederates mounted a countercharge. It "was made in the grand style," observed one eyewitness, Dr. Lewis H. Steiner, an inspector for the U.S. Sanitary Commission who had been trapped in Frederick during the Confederate occupation. "Saddles were emptied on both sides."

The Federal cannon managed to get off only one round before the charging Confederates knocked it into a ditch. As suddenly as it began, the little skirmish ended. While the Federal infantry rushed at the double-quick into one end of town, Hampton's Confederates trotted out the other end with a dozen prisoners, including the over-eager Colonel Moor. Confederate Captain William Blackford also carried an additional prize, a freshly baked plum cake, which had been presented to him under fire by a woman as a parting gift.

The citizens of Frederick had hardly suffered under the brief Confederate occupation, but they loyally welcomed the Federals as liberators. General Cox, who led his Kanawha Division into town, wrote that "whilst the carbine smoke and the smell of powder still lingered, the closed window-shutters of the houses flew open, the sashes went up, the windows were filled with ladies waving their handkerchiefs and national flags, whilst the men came to the column with fruits and refreshments."

McClellan, who arrived in Frederick with the main body of the army about 9 a.m. the following day, was mobbed — "nearly pulled to pieces," he wrote his wife, Ellen. Crying and laughing, women thrust out their babies to the general and hugged his horse, Dan Webster. They kissed his uniform and covered both McClellan and his mount with

Federal foragers return to their camp in the Maryland countryside with a rich haul of cattle and poultry. "Whether the natives sold to us gladly or not," a Federal soldier wrote, "they had much to sell, so our march was pleasant."

wreaths and flowers. Someone in the crowd inserted in the bridle of Dan Webster a little American flag, which the general later sent to his wife.

Much as McClellan loved all the attention, it would pale beside the gift bestowed upon him later that morning by a pair of soldiers from the 27th Indiana. Shortly before 10 a.m. on Saturday, the 27th stopped at a meadow on the outskirts of Frederick for a rest break.

Sergeant John M. Bloss and Corporal Barton W. Mitchell of Company F lounged in the grass, looking idly around them. It was evident that this same meadow had served as a campground for the Confederates a few days before. Mitchell's gaze lit upon something in the tall grass nearby. It turned out to be a kind of package — three cigars wrapped in a sheet of paper.

Free cigars were a happy discovery, but the wrapper was also intriguing. It was addressed to Confederate General D. H. Hill and bore the heading, "Special Orders No. 191, Headquarters, Army of Northern Virginia." Mitchell had found the extra copy of the Confederate plan of operation.

Mitchell and Bloss took their discovery to the company commander, who quickly sent it up the chain of command. The division adjutant general, Samuel E. Pittman, immediately realized that the document must be authentic; he recognized the familiar handwriting of Lee's adjutant general, Robert H. Chilton, a comrade from the prewar Army.

Pittman went all the way to the top, to McClellan's headquarters at the edge of Frederick. McClellan was conferring with a delegation of Frederick businessmen when Pittman requested immediate admission to the commanding general's tent.

McClellan unfolded the paper and read it with rising excitement. Here, spelled out in detail, were the whereabouts and objectives of each command in Lee's army. Suddenly all those conflicting pieces of intelligence McClellan had been receiving fell into place — Lee had divided his army.

When he finished reading, McClellan threw up his arms and exclaimed, "Now I know what to do!"

McClellan had on his desk a telegram, one of the latest in a series of anxious queries from President Lincoln: "How does it look now?"

At noon, McClellan telegraphed his elated reply: "I have the whole rebel force in front of me, but I am confident, and no time shall be lost. I think Lee has made a gross mistake, and that he will be severely punished for it. I have all the plans of the rebels, and will catch them in their own trap if my men are equal to the emergency. Will send you trophies."

Passing through Frederick on his powerful bay, Dan Webster, General George B. McClellan touches the hand of a child thrust up to greet him. "The whole population turned out, wild with joy," a Federal officer wrote. "When McClellan appeared, the crowd became so demonstrative that we were forcibly brought to a halt."

A covered railroad bridge spans the Potomac at Harpers Ferry in 1859.

A Vulnerable Federal Garrison

In September 1862, the picturesque hamlet of Harpers Ferry became a target for seizure by Robert E. Lee's Army of Northern Virginia. It was a familiar role for the little town at the confluence of the Potomac and Shenandoah Rivers. John Brown's raid on its arsenal in 1859 had thrust the place into prominence, and its strategic position at the northern entrance to the Shenandoah Valley and astride the Baltimore & Ohio Railroad ensured its importance in the ensuing conflict. Already it had changed hands twice: In April 1861, the Federals gave way to the Confederates. In June 1861, the Confederates withdrew, and their foe returned.

The vulnerability of Harpers Ferry was guaranteed by the surrounding terrain. Dominated by mountainous bluffs from which an attacker could rain down shot and shell, the town was practically indefensible. "We were at the bottom of a bowl," a Federal defender recalled. "The dullest soldier could see the inevitable result." Small wonder that Stonewall Jackson maintained he would rather "take the place 40 times than undertake to defend it once."

In this 1862 photograph, the Federals at Harpers Ferry have begun construction of a

pontoon bridge alongside the railroad bridge, damaged the year before as the town changed hands. The arsenal *(foreground)* was burned and abandoned in 1861 as well.

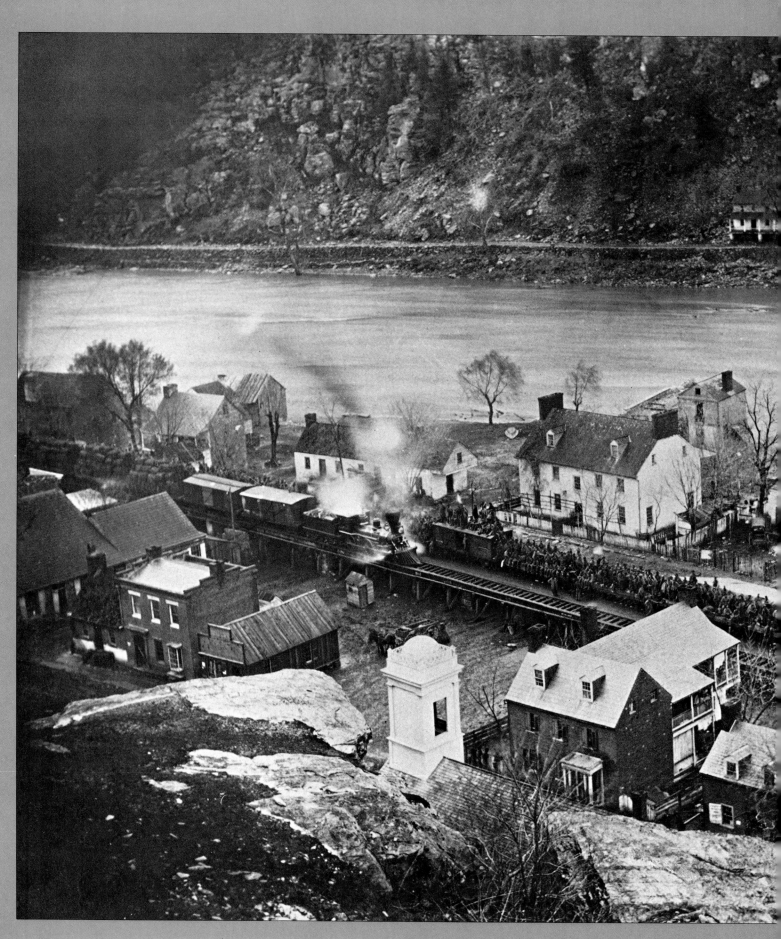

Crowded aboard railway flatcars, Ohio troops pause in Harpers Ferry as a supply train chugs through town on the adjacent track. The B & O Railroad was the most important route for Federal reinforcements traveling to and from the West.

U.S. Army tents occupy the grounds around the old Federal arsenal buildings at Harpers Ferry in 1862. Most of the local populace had fled the previous year, leaving the once-prosperous town all but deserted.

Company A of the 22nd New York Militia, part of a 12,000-man contingent guarding Harpers Ferry, drills on the heights above the town in September 1862.

The B & O Railroad bridge, repaired by the Federals in the summer of 1862, crosses the Potomac toward Harpers Ferry. The span was rebuilt nine times during the War.

Clash at South Mountain

"The vast army of McClellan spread out before me. The marching columns extended back as far as eye could see in the distance. It was a grand and glorious spectacle, and it was impossible to look at it without admiration."

GENERAL D. H. HILL, C.S.A., AT THE BATTLE OF SOUTH MOUNTAIN

The lost copy of Lee's order that came into Federal hands on Saturday, September 13, 1862, described to the letter the actual dispositions of the divided Confederate forces — with one exception. According to the order, Longstreet's wing was supposed to halt at Boonsboro, 15 miles northwest of McClellan's headquarters at Frederick. But by September 10, Lee — who was with Longstreet — had heard a report that Federals from Pennsylvania were marching south toward Hagerstown. Since Hagerstown was to be the springboard for Lee's invasion of Pennsylvania, he and Longstreet went to that city with 10,000 men, leaving only D. H. Hill's division of 5,000 men at Boonsboro to guard the rear.

Thus, Lee's 50,000 troops were actually deployed in five separate forces instead of four, spread out over 25 miles, providing McClellan with an even greater opportunity than he imagined. That Saturday afternoon, waving the copy of Lee's order, McClellan exulted to one of his brigadiers, "Here is a paper with which if I cannot whip Bobbie Lee, I will be willing to go home."

For both Lee and McClellan, the Federal garrison at Harpers Ferry was the key — and time the crucial factor. Lee needed a quick victory there so that his dangerously divided forces could reunite before the Army of the Potomac caught up with them. McClellan wanted the garrison to hold out as long as possible, to allow him, as he wrote, to "cut the enemy in two and beat him in detail" — one piece at a time.

The command of Harpers Ferry had been entrusted to Colonel Dixon S. Miles, a gray-bearded veteran of 38 years in the U.S. Army. Miles was a native Marylander who had fought with distinction during the Mexican War and against Indians on the frontier. On the eve of the Civil War, he had ranked among the top 30 officers in the Army. But his fondness for alcohol had since taken its toll. Given command of a division at the First Battle of Bull Run, he rode about in excited confusion — under the influence, it was said, of brandy prescribed by his doctor for an illness. A military court of inquiry determined that Miles had indeed been drunk. He swore off liquor and was shipped to Harpers Ferry.

Miles had orders from General in Chief Halleck to defend Harpers Ferry to "the latest moment." His garrison numbered about 14,000 men, many of them inexperienced. They included 2,500 troops who on September 11 had been forced out of Martinsburg, 15 miles to the northwest, by the approach of Stonewall Jackson's three divisions.

The converging Confederate forces were, in the main, veterans — and they outnumbered the Harpers Ferry garrison by more than 7,000 men. Furthermore, Harpers Ferry was hemmed in by high ground, terrain that vastly favored the attackers. West of town, the ground rose gradually for about a mile and a half to Bolivar Heights, a 668-foot-high plateau that stretched from the Po-

This sword and scabbard were worn by 31-year-old Brigadier General Samuel Garland Jr. in the battle for South Mountain on September 14, 1862. Garland was killed as he tried to rally his North Carolina regiments against a Federal division attacking Fox's Gap.

tomac River to the Shenandoah River. South of town, just across the Shenandoah, loomed Loudoun Heights, 1,180 feet high. And across the Potomac to the north towered the 1,476-foot-high crest of Maryland Heights, the southernmost extremity of 12-mile-long Elk Ridge. The Federals had to hold these eminences, especially the dominant crest of Maryland Heights. Otherwise, wrote a Federal soldier, Harpers Ferry would be "no more defensible than a well bottom."

Yet Colonel Miles assumed that since the western approach to Harpers Ferry was comparatively level, the Confederates would attack from that direction. He ignored Loudoun Heights altogether, and put a force of only 2,000 men on the most important position of all, Maryland Heights.

On the night of Thursday, September 11, about 8,000 Confederates under General Lafayette McLaws arrived at Brownsville, six miles northeast of Harpers Ferry in Pleasant Valley, bounded on the east by South Mountain and on the west by Elk Ridge.

On the following day, McLaws deployed his troops methodically. He left 3,000 men near Brownsville Gap in South Mountain to protect his rear. He moved 3,000 others toward the Potomac to seal off the eastern escape route from Harpers Ferry. Finally, he assigned the crucial task of seizing Maryland Heights to the veteran brigades of Brigadier Generals Joseph Kershaw and William Barksdale. They were to mount Elk Ridge at a pass called Solomon's Gap, then turn south, march four miles along the ridge and drive the Federal defenders off the crest overlooking Harpers Ferry.

Early that day, with Kershaw's South Carolinians in the lead, the Confederates ascended Solomon's Gap with little opposition, brushing aside a detachment of about 40 Federals. The terrain they encountered along the crest of the ridge proved a tougher obstacle. As they moved south, the Confederates followed a path so narrow that they had to grab at bushes and trees to keep from tumbling down the slope. At 6 p.m., after moving less than four miles, they ran into a Federal abatis, and a volley of musketry from behind the felled trees stopped them for the night.

The following morning, September 13, Kershaw's men drove back the Federals and

From an outpost atop Maryland Heights, Federal soldiers survey the town of Harpers Ferry, Virginia, bordered by the Potomac River *(right)* and the Shenandoah

River. In the distance, tents carpet the high plateau known as Bolivar Heights, where the Federals concentrated their defenses.

advanced about 400 yards before running into a second, larger abatis guarding Maryland Heights. Just beyond this barrier, and only about a mile from the ridge overlooking Harpers Ferry, stood a crude breastwork of stones and logs that the Federals had hastily erected across the crest.

Behind the breastwork were massed 1,700 troops, a force nearly equal to the two attacking Confederate brigades. But the Federals were ill-prepared. In the center of a defense line that included Ohio, Maryland and Rhode Island recruits was the green 126th New York, a regiment that had been raised only three weeks previously. In addition, the Federals' seven artillery pieces, including two powerful 10-inch Dahlgrens, were sited to cover the southern and western approaches to Harpers Ferry and hence were useless against an attack from the north. Nor were the defenders fortunate in their commander, Colonel Thomas H. Ford of the 32nd Ohio. Ford had been a successful Ohio politician, but had limited military ability. This morning he did not feel well, and he elected to stay back two miles behind the lines, leaving the fighting to Colonel Eliakim Sherrill, the ranking officer on the ridge.

Kershaw had begun his attack at about 6:30 a.m. His plan was to push his own brigade directly against the abatis while Barksdale's Mississippians flanked the Federal right farther down the slope where the going was easier. Twice Kershaw's Confederates charged into the abatis, and twice they were driven back with heavy losses.

The inexperienced New Yorkers were holding their own. They were heartened by the courageous example of Colonel Sherrill, a former U.S. Congressman. Sherrill's only military experience had been in the peace-

time militia, but now he was striding back and forth recklessly, waving his revolver and exhorting his young soldiers. When the Confederates charged again, Sherrill jumped up on the breastwork for a better view. A Minié ball tore through his cheek, mangling his tongue.

After Sherrill was carried off the field, the New Yorkers grew panicky. To their right, on the eastern slope of the ridge, Barksdale's brigade of Mississippians had scrambled along the lower slope of the ridge, flanking the abatis and the breastwork. Rumors of an order to retreat circulated through the ranks of the New Yorkers, and the green troops broke and fled rearward, stampeding down the south slope toward Harpers Ferry and trying desperately to take cover behind rocks and bushes. Major Sylvester Hewitt, Colonel Ford's aide, ordered the remaining units to withdraw from the breastwork and re-form farther along the ridge.

Up from Harpers Ferry to stem the retreat came Colonel Miles. At length, he and other officers managed to stop the flight of the 126th but were unable to calm the troops and rally them. For some reason, neither Miles nor Ford thought to send forward the 900 men of the 115th New York, who were waiting in reserve midway up the south slope.

At 3:30 p.m., outnumbered and threatened from front and flank, Ford ordered a total withdrawal from Maryland Heights. The big guns were spiked, and several of them were shoved off the ridge. By 4:30 p.m., all of Ford's troops had retreated down the mountain and across the pontoon bridge over the Potomac into Harpers Ferry, leaving Maryland Heights to the enemy. The decision to withdraw would haunt Ford. He insisted that Miles had given him the author-

ity to do so, but a court of inquiry would later conclude that he had "abandoned his position without sufficient cause," and would recommend his dismissal from the Army.

Earlier on the 13th, the two other Confederate wings had arrived and moved into position. John Walker's 3,400-man division reached the base of Loudoun Heights about 10 a.m. To their astonishment, the Confederates found not a single Federal soldier there. An hour after Walker's arrival, Stonewall Jackson approached Harpers Ferry from the west with three divisions and deployed his 11,500 men a couple of miles from Bolivar Heights, where the Federals had their main defenses.

The arrival of Walker and Jackson completed the Confederate encirclement. In Harpers Ferry, Federal officers were fully aware of their predicament. That night, Miles's subordinates begged him to attempt to recapture Maryland Heights. Miles refused, insisting that his forces remain along Bolivar Heights to defend the town from the west. He exclaimed stubbornly, "I am ordered to hold this place and God damn my soul to hell if I don't."

The fact that Miles took such a literal view of his orders — to hold Harpers Ferry and the nearby Bolivar Heights but not the crucial high ground to the north and south — was only one of the things that puzzled and frustrated his subordinates. Though no one could say for sure that Miles had taken to the bottle again, his officers sensed in their commander an alarming mental confusion.

During the night, Miles summoned Captain Charles Russell of the 1st Maryland Cavalry and ordered him to take nine horsemen and break through the enemy encirclement. Russell was to ride through enemy lines to

McClellan's headquarters, 20 miles northeast of Harpers Ferry, and inform the general that the besieged town could hold out for 48 hours. After that, Miles said, he would have to surrender.

In fact, McClellan already knew that Harpers Ferry was under siege. His signal stations on hills to the south of Frederick reported hearing the sounds of battle that Saturday afternoon.

McClellan had spent the afternoon developing his plan of attack. He intended to relieve Harpers Ferry and to pounce upon the scattered pieces of the Confederate army where they were pinpointed in Lee's order. To accomplish those goals, he first would have to get his big army across the barriers presented by Catoctin Mountain, just west of Frederick, and the more formidable South Mountain, a dozen miles beyond. Actually a ridge rather than a single peak, South Mountain extended roughly 50 miles from the Potomac north into Pennsylvania. This long wall, reaching heights of up to 1,600 feet, was pierced by two principal passes: Turner's Gap, where the National Road from Frederick crossed the ridge en route to Boonsboro at the western base of the mountain; and Crampton's Gap, six miles to the south, where the Burkittsville Road debouched into Pleasant Valley, the back door to Harpers Ferry. A smaller pass, Fox's Gap, crossed the mountain about a mile south of Turner's Gap.

At 6:20 p.m., six hours after coming into possession of Lee's order, McClellan began issuing his own orders for Sunday morning's march. Most of the Army of the Potomac — 79,000 men encamped near Frederick and at Middletown farther west — would follow the National Road toward Turner's Gap. Their target was the Confederate force at Boonsboro — which McClellan mistakenly believed from Lee's order to be the bulk of the Confederate army. The remainder of the Army of the Potomac consisted of about 12,000 men under Major General William Franklin at Buckeystown, six miles south of Frederick; and Major General Darius Couch's 7,200-man division, five miles farther south at Licksville. Together, they were to cross South Mountain at Crampton's Gap, cut off the Confederates besieging Harpers Ferry, and relieve the garrison.

Nothing had happened to change McClellan's misconceptions about the strength of Lee's scattered forces. He still thought they totaled 120,000 men. And he still believed that Longstreet and D. H. Hill were together at Boonsboro, not separated by 13 miles.

Up at Hagerstown that night, Robert E. Lee received two alarming dispatches. Jeb Stuart at Turner's Gap reported that a Southern sympathizer from Frederick had slipped through the Federal lines to tell a disturbing story. The man had been among the delegation of Frederick citizens present that morning when the lost order was brought to McClellan. Seeing McClellan's excited reaction, he surmised that a major piece of intelligence must have fallen into Federal hands. In another message, D. H. Hill reported from Boonsboro that an enormous number of Federal campfires were ablaze around Middletown, four miles east of Turner's Gap.

Lee quickly took precautions to meet the threat. He fired off messages to McLaws and Jackson urging them to hurry up with their siege of Harpers Ferry and warning that McClellan might attempt to relieve the Federal garrison there. Then, to gain time for the completion of the Harpers Ferry operation, he ordered a full-scale defense of Turner's Gap. "The gap must be held at all hazards," he told Stuart. D. H. Hill was to support Stuart's cavalry there. And to provide additional manpower, Lee ordered Longstreet to march from Hagerstown to Turner's Gap at daybreak with eight of his nine brigades.

Sunday, September 14, dawned bright and hot as long columns of Federals converged on South Mountain. In the forefront of the Federal advance against Turner's Gap was a IX Corps division of 3,000 Ohioans and West Virginians led by Brigadier General Jacob Cox.

When Cox broke camp at 6 a.m., he understood that the mission of his two brigades was merely to support a cavalry reconnaissance by Brigadier General Alfred Pleasonton. Soon, however, he learned that trouble lay ahead. He came upon a familiar figure standing by the road. It was Colonel Augustus Moor, his impetuous brigade commander, who had been captured by the Confederate cavalry two days before in the little skirmish at Frederick. Moor explained that he had been paroled and was making his way back to the Federal lines. When Cox told him that the troops were headed for Turner's Gap, Moor gave a start and exclaimed, "My God! Be careful." Then, remembering that the terms of his parole forbade supplying intelligence, Moor turned away. Thus forewarned, Cox ordered up his second brigade and sent a message to alert the commander of IX Corps, Major General Jesse Reno.

At Bolivar, a crossroads at the eastern base of South Mountain, Cox and Pleasonton decided not to attack through Turner's Gap but to flank whatever Confederates defended the summit there. They turned onto the Old Sharpsburg Road, which crossed the mountain at Fox's Gap, south of Turner's Gap.

Cox's men began the two-mile climb up the steep slope. Just short of the crest, they reached an open field. At the far edge were a Confederate cavalry detachment of 200 men and a 1,000-man brigade of North Carolinians under Brigadier General Samuel Garland Jr., a 31-year-old Virginian and one of Lee's most promising commanders. Garland had selected a strong position behind portions of a stone wall bordering a road that ran along the mountain crest from Turner's Gap to Fox's Gap.

About 9 a.m. both sides opened up with artillery and musketry, and soon the fighting raged all along the line. One of Cox's brigade commanders, Colonel Eliakim Scammon, made up his mind to flank the southern end of the Confederate defenses. He ordered the 23rd Ohio to move through dense woods to the left. The 23rd's commander, Lieutenant Colonel Rutherford B. Hayes, led his men through the woods and then up the slope. "Give them hell!" he shouted. "Give the sons of bitches hell!" Near the crest, as Hayes was urging his men on, a musketball struck his left arm. Faint with pain, Hayes sank to the ground still shouting orders. As the bedlam of battle swirled around him, Hayes realized at length that next to him lay a wounded Confederate. The pain was so great, and the enemy firing so intense, that Hayes feared he might not survive. He gave the Confederate a message to take to his wife, Lucy, in the event he died there.

As it happened, Hayes did survive, with a severe fracture. And while he was being carried to safety, his Ohioans gained the summit

and turned the Confederate right, at a cost of 130 casualties, including 32 killed.

The Confederates now had to face assaults from the right and the front, but they were still full of fight. When Colonel Scammon ordered two guns from the 1st Ohio Battery up into the open field within 40 yards of the Confederate line, the defenders began picking off the gunners one by one. But the men who fell were replaced, and the Federals continued to rake the Confederates with canister. In the center of the line, the 12th Ohio stormed over the stone wall, and the foes went at it hand to hand; bayonets flashed and muskets became clubs.

The Confederate commander, General Garland, galloped to the left of his line where the 13th North Carolina, under Colonel Thomas Ruffin, was hotly engaged. No sooner had Garland conferred with Ruffin about the dangerous situation than Ruffin took a hit in the hip and went down. Seconds later, Ruffin heard a groan and turned to see Garland mortally wounded and writhing in pain. Soon Garland was dead.

Demoralized by the loss of their commander, hard-pressed in the center and flanked on their right, the North Carolinians fell back in disarray down the west slope of the mountain, losing 200 prisoners to the onrushing Ohioans.

By 11 a.m. Cox commanded Fox's Gap. His division, weary after two hours of bitter combat, pushed north on the road running along the ridge toward the National Road at Turner's Gap. On leaving Fox's Gap, the Federals passed by the farm of Daniel Wise, into whose well the rapidly decaying bodies of more than 60 Confederate dead would be dumped for quick disposal. The Federals would compensate Wise — at a dollar a head.

At Turner's Gap, D. H. Hill, the Confederate division commander, felt the world closing in. Earlier that day, he had climbed a lookout station near the Mountain House, an old inn at the crest of the gap, and gasped at the awesome panorama of McClellan's seemingly endless columns marching west from Middletown. Now came the devastating news of Garland's death and the decimation of his North Carolina brigade. Hill had only one other brigade on the mountain, and it was needed to guard the immediate vicinity of Turner's Gap. He later wrote, "I do not remember ever to have experienced a feeling of greater *loneliness*."

To meet the threat of Cox's Federals advancing from Fox's Gap, Hill had to take immediate action. But with what? His three other brigades had not yet completed the three-mile march from Boonsboro; Longstreet's eight brigades were on the way from Hagerstown but still hours away. So Daniel Harvey Hill staged a desperate ruse. He ran two guns south along the ridge road and mustered what he described as "a line of dismounted staff-officers, couriers, teamsters and cooks to give the appearance of battery supports." Near a farm the guns opened on the Federals with canister, plowing up furrows in the fields with a sound, Cox observed, "like the cutting of a melon rind."

This fearsome display stalled the Federals, and soon the timely arrival of one of Hill's brigades from Boonsboro stopped the advance altogether. Toward noon, pressed by the Confederates, Cox pulled his tired troops back to Fox's Gap and waited for reinforcements.

McClellan, who had not expected the Confederates to give battle until his vanguard crossed the mountain to Boonsboro, spent

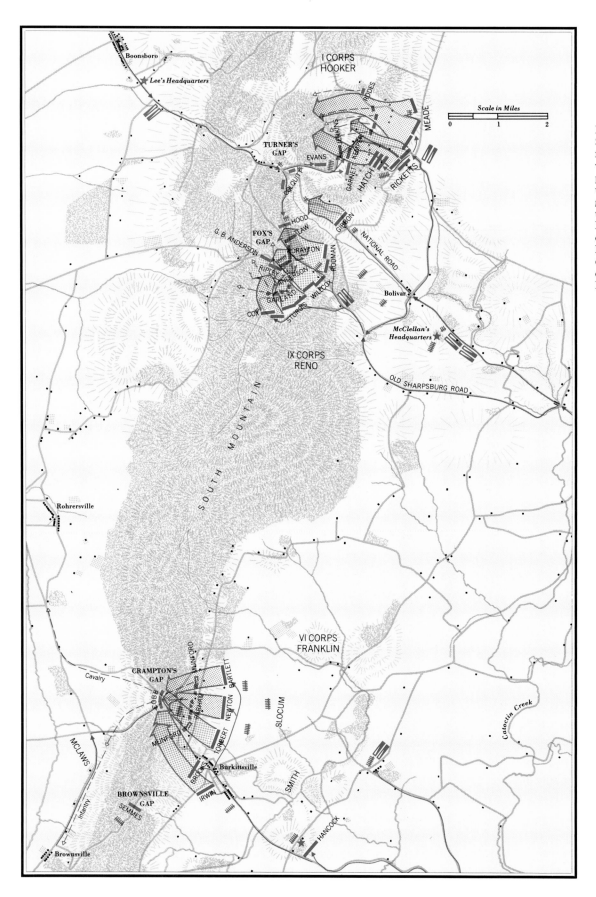

In the battle for South Mountain on September 14, the outnumbered Confederates contested McClellan's westward advance at three key passes. At Turner's Gap, a handful of understrength Confederate brigades gave ground before three divisions under Joseph Hooker. At Fox's Gap, D. H. Hill's troops held off the four divisions of Jesse Reno's IX Corps. But at Crampton's Gap, the Confederate defenders were forced to withdraw before the onslaught of William Franklin's 12,000-man VI Corps.

the morning at his Frederick headquarters. When two young aides alerted him that a major battle was under way around Turner's Gap, he hurried forward to the headquarters of Major General Ambrose Burnside, commander of the right wing, on a knoll near the foot of South Mountain.

McClellan's presence seemed to galvanize his troops. He sat on his horse at the roadside, and the passing columns of men cheered him as they marched toward the battle. A Federal soldier wrote: "It seemed as if an intermission had been declared in order that a reception might be tendered to the general in chief. The general pointed with his finger to the gap in the mountain through which our path lay. It was like a great scene in a play, with the roar of the guns for an accompaniment."

The progress of the Federal troops massed in the valley was painfully slow. "Each column was a monstrous, crawling blue-black snake miles long," wrote David L. Thompson of the 9th New York. The lull in the fighting had lasted nearly three hours when the first Federal reinforcements, Brigadier General Orlando Willcox's division, reached Fox's Gap and went into action against Hill's men just to the north sometime after 2 p.m.

One of Willcox's regiments, the 17th Michigan, was facing fire for the first time. The 500 Michigan men were so raw, said one, that they did not even know the "rudiments of military maneuvering." Soon they found themselves seeking cover behind an open rail fence while the Confederates, crouching behind a stone wall 80 yards away, kept up a steady fire. But when the order to charge came, the Michiganders mustered an extra measure of courage. They raged across an open field and drove the enemy away from the wall and into the woods. It was a costly baptism, with 30 dead and about 100 wounded, but the word went down the line that they had "fought like tigers."

D. H. Hill still had only a pair of brigades to face the Federal reinforcements at Fox's Gap. These outnumbered Confederates could see yet additional columns of Federals tramping up the Old Sharpsburg Road — two divisions of Reno's corps. By 3 p.m., Hill's exhausted men teetered on the brink of collapse. Some of them had been in line for nearly six hours.

Then, at the last moment, help arrived in the form of Longstreet's vanguard, which came into view about 3:30. The men were dusty and tired after a 13-mile march over rough terrain that had taken them 19 hours.

As Longstreet's troops approached the western base of the mountain, they were cheered by the sight of Robert E. Lee. He was astride Traveller again, though his hands were still bandaged and an aide had to hold the reins. Filing by Lee, the troops of Hood's division became agitated. They began to shout for their commander, John Bell Hood, who was still under arrest in the dispute with General Nathan Evans over ownership of those Federal wagons captured at Second Bull Run.

"Give us Hood!" they yelled.

Lee raised his hat and answered, "You shall have him, gentlemen."

Lee sent for Hood and offered to restore his command if he would express regret over the incident. Hood refused and started to argue his case again. "Well," Lee interrupted, "I will suspend your arrest till the impending battle is decided."

With his men shouting their approval, Hood led the division toward Fox's Gap. He

arrived there in time to plug a big hole in the Confederate line. Thus bolstered, the defenders were able to stave off repeated Federal attempts to crack through on the ridge.

Trying to break the stalemate, General Reno rode forward at sundown for a personal reconnaissance. Reno was astride his horse in one of farmer Wise's fields, not far from the spot where Confederate General Samuel Garland had fallen that morning, when the woods erupted with gunfire and a bullet tore into him.

As Reno was being carried to the rear, he hailed one of his division commanders, Brigadier General Samuel Sturgis. "Hallo, Sam, I'm dead!" Reno called out in a tone so firm and cheerful that Sturgis could not believe he was seriously hurt. Minutes later, Reno died.

Thus far the Federals had made no serious attempt to force Turner's Gap or flank it on the north. At 4 p.m., McClellan finally moved up Major General Joseph Hooker's I Corps, which had marched all day from their bivouac on the far side of Frederick. McClellan ordered Hooker's entire corps except one

Fierce fighting around the Wise farmhouse, situated on the fence-lined Old Sharpsburg Road at Fox's Gap, took the lives of Federal General Jesse Reno (*right, top*) and Confederate General Samuel Garland (*bottom*). Confederate General D. H. Hill claimed that Garland had "no superiors and few equals in the service," but called the Southern-born Reno "a renegade Virginian, killed by a happy shot from the 23rd North Carolina."

brigade to make a wide flanking movement around to the north. The unit he held back was the so-called Black Hat Brigade of Brigadier General John Gibbon, which had fought with distinction at the Second Battle of Bull Run. Gibbon was ordered to march his men straight up the National Road and deliver a head-on attack at Turner's Gap.

Gibbon lined up a pair of 12-pounder Napoleon cannon in the roadway, formed his regiments in columns, two on either side of the road, and started up the gorge. Quickly the Federals came under fire from enemy skirmishers. "For half a mile of advance," wrote Major Rufus Dawes of the Black Hat Brigade's 6th Wisconsin, "our skirmishers played a deadly game of 'Bo-peep,' hiding behind logs, fences, rocks and bushes."

Confederate artillery opened up from the summit, but the Federals did not falter, even when a shell exploded amidst the 2nd Wisconsin, killing or wounding nine men. The brigade's extraordinary poise won praise from McClellan, who was watching through field glasses a mile or so to the rear.

About dusk, Gibbon's brigade approached the main body of Confederates near the crest and swung into line of battle. The defenders — mostly Georgia men — were deployed several hundred yards below the summit, where the pass narrows. They waited behind a stone wall and in a ditch to the north of the road, and on a wooded hillside south of it. The troops, a brigade of five regiments under Alfred Colquitt, newly promoted to brigadier general, had seen little action all day. They held their fire until the Federals were only 40 yards from the stone wall. Then the Confederates let loose a volley, and the battle was joined.

Soon it grew so dark that the Federals had to take aim, wrote Dawes, "by the flashes of the enemy's guns." At length, Dawes and the 6th Wisconsin worked their way up the hillside to the right of the Confederate-held wall. But Colquitt's men met them there, repulsing charge after charge and bringing cries of "Hurrah for Georgia!" from D. H. Hill's staff officers in the rear.

By 9 p.m., Colquitt had lost 100 men and Gibbon 318 — one fourth of his brigade. Both sides were low on ammunition, and the deadly spits of flame that had lit the gorge like fireflies subsided.

Meanwhile, as the Georgians kept a tenacious grip on Turner's Gap, Confederates to the north faced overwhelming odds. Brigadier General Robert Rodes with his brigade of 1,200 Alabamians had to cover a difficult spur of the mountain that extended north from the National Road, dipping into a ravine and then rising to a commanding peak nearly a mile away. Earlier in the day, he had deployed four regiments on this peak and the fifth one on the lower ground closer to the road. Between the contingents he left a gap, to be filled by three small brigades of Longstreet's troops when they arrived later.

Coming at Rodes's brigade were two divisions from Hooker's I Corps. As the Federals began their advance up the steep slope sometime after 4 p.m., they covered such a wide front that Rodes reported he was flanked by a half mile on either side. To slow the Federals, Rodes pushed his skirmishers down into the woods near the base of the mountain.

On Rodes's right, the Federal division under Brigadier General John Hatch quickly cleared away the skirmishers and advanced along the Old Hagerstown Road, which ran through the ravine separating Rodes's Confederates. Near the ridge, Hatch's men be-

came engaged in a fierce contest before a fence at the edge of a cornfield. Hatch fell severely wounded and was succeeded by Brigadier General Abner Doubleday. As a ruse, Doubleday ordered his men to cease firing and lie down quietly behind the fence. The trick worked. The 26th Alabama sprang forward only to meet a sudden sweeping volley from the hidden Federals that sent them rushing backward, leaving their dead alongside the fence.

On Rodes's left the Federal threat was even greater. The Pennsylvania Reserve Division of Brigadier General George Meade, swinging to the north, pressed the Confederate flank vigorously. The twin Federal assaults cost Rodes a third of his brigade — 422 men dead, wounded or captured — and he grudgingly yielded the high peak. By dark, he had given up perhaps a half mile of his original line and was being squeezed back upon Colquitt's position in Turner's Gap.

As the victorious Federals pursued Rodes's battered regiments, they encountered Longstreet's three small brigades coming up to fill the gap in the Confederate line. After a sharp fight, these Confederates also gave way. One regiment, the 19th Virginia, lost its colonel and 63 of 150 men. But darkness put an end to the struggle.

Down at Crampton's Gap, six miles to the south, a second crucial battle had been waged on that bloody Sunday. William Franklin's VI Corps, with its vital mission of breaking through to the besieged garrison at Harpers Ferry, approached the gap about noon. Franklin was late and had only two divisions; en route from camp at Buckeystown, he had wasted time waiting in vain for

As dusk settles over South Mountain, Federals of John Hatch's division overrun Alabama troops firing from behind stone outcroppings on the wooded crest north of Turner's Gap.

a third division, that of General Couch, which would unaccountably fail to show up until 10 p.m.

Entering Burkittsville, a mile or so southeast of the gap, Franklin's men came under fire from Confederate artillery. "Through the street we went," wrote Major Thomas W. Hyde of the 7th Maine, "while cannon balls crashed among the houses, and the women, young and old, with great coolness, waved their handkerchiefs and flags at us."

At the eastern base of the mountain, below Crampton's Gap, a handful of Confederate infantry and three dismounted cavalry regiments, all commanded by Colonel Thomas T. Munford, lay behind a line of stone walls and rail fences along a farm lane jutting north from the Burkittsville Road. Two batteries of artillery were posted on the slope. Altogether, the Confederates had no more than

1,000 men. They watched awe-struck while Franklin's force approached from Burkittsville. Even without Couch's division, the Federals outnumbered the Confederates by better than 12 to 1. Back up the slope, George Neese, a gunner in the Confederate horse artillery, observed that the Federals "were so numerous that it looked as if they were creeping up out of the ground." But Neese also noted the extraordinary caution of the Federals, who reminded him of "a lion, making exceedingly careful preparations to spring on a plucky little mouse."

The main Federal assault began a little after 3 p.m. on a front more than a mile wide. Major General Henry Slocum's division moved head on against the Confederates, while two brigades of Major General William F. Smith's division advanced south of the Burkittsville Road to flank the enemy right.

Sheets of Federal fire ripped through the ranks of the outmanned defenders, and soon the fence row was lined with dead and wounded Confederates. George Bernard of the 12th Virginia caught a ball in the right leg. A comrade wrapped a leather strap around the leg to stanch the bleeding. Then, while bullets whizzed through the rail fence, Bernard lay on his side behind the fence's low stone footing "with arms and legs drawn about as close to my body as was possible, well knowing that I could not afford to occupy one inch of superfluous space." After a while, sparks from the muzzles of Federal rifles ignited dry leaves. The fire spread to the wooden fence rails, and Bernard had to drag himself away.

Colonel Alfred Torbert then shouted to his New Jersey Brigade to charge the Confederates. "We bounded forward with a cheer," recalled Sergeant John Beach of the 4th New Jersey. The attackers captured a number of men, including Bernard, and forced the remainder of the Confederates up the mountainside.

During the pursuit up the slope, there were dozens of confused skirmishes — and at least one instance of high pragmatism. A Vermont soldier, trying to climb a ledge, slipped and tumbled into a crevice only to find that a Confederate rifleman had preceded him there. The enemies glared at each other. Then the Confederate burst out laughing. "We're both in a fix," he reasoned. "You can't gobble me, and I can't gobble you. Let's wait till the shooting is over, and if your side wins I'm your prisoner, and if we win you're my prisoner."

Even as this bargain was struck, the outcome was being decided at the crest of Crampton's Gap.

Colonel Thomas T. Munford of the 2nd Virginia Cavalry, commanding the small force assigned to defend Crampton's Gap, had exhorted his officers to "hold the post at all hazards." But the Federal assault routed both Munford's men and General Howell Cobb's reinforcements, whom Munford spotted "running in great disorder on the Harpers Ferry road, followed a short distance by the enemy."

Prominent in the Federal assault on the summit was the 4th New Jersey, a regiment that had recently lost its original brigade commander, Philip Kearny, slain two weeks before at Chantilly. During the assault, the 4th New Jersey's Sergeant Jacob Ostermann shouted Kearny's name, and it seemed to spur the men to rare ferocity. Against them, the Confederates on the summit could make only a brief stand; then they broke and fled down the western slope. The New Jerseyans, who had lost their regimental colors to the Confederates at Gaines's Mill during the Seven Days' Battles, captured two stands of colors and salvaged enough Springfield rifles abandoned by the fleeing enemy to replace all their old smoothbore muskets.

Confederate reinforcements — the two lead regiments of Brigadier General Howell Cobb's 1,300-man brigade — ascended the western slope only to be swept up in the rush to the rear. Cobb grabbed a regimental flag and attempted to rally his men, an act as useless, Colonel Munford observed, as attempting "to rally a flock of frightened sheep." A Federal bullet shattered the flagstaff, and Cobb gave it up, following his troops in their retreat to the base of the mountain. There, a mile or so from the crest, in Pleasant Valley, waited General McLaws — who had hurried north from Mary-

land Heights with seven regiments. McLaws patched together a new line from these reinforcements and the remnants left over from the battle in the gap.

It was about 6 p.m. In three hours of hard fighting, the Federals had seized Crampton's Gap, taking 500 casualties against 750 for the Confederates. Harpers Ferry lay only six miles away. Franklin might well have pushed on. In his orders, McClellan had asked him to use all the "intellect and the utmost activity that a general can exercise" in order to relieve Harpers Ferry. But instead of pushing resolutely on, Franklin probed cautiously at McLaws' improvised line in Pleasant Valley. Then he decided that his men had had enough and ordered them to bed down for the night on the mountain.

Pondering the dismal events of the day, Lee decided to withdraw from Turner's Gap. With the Federals holding the high ground and with thousands of reinforcements waiting to attack, the pass would be impossible to defend come daylight. In the night, the remaining troops of Longstreet and Hill began their retreat down the western slope. They were under orders to march toward Sharpsburg, six miles to the west. The defense of the South Mountain gaps had proved costly to the Confederates; of the roughly 18,000 men engaged, they had lost 2,700, including 800 missing. The Federals had thrown in more than 28,000 troops and had lost 1,800.

"The day has gone against us," Lee wrote in a dispatch to McLaws at 8 p.m. Then he added a startling notation: He had decided not to stop at Sharpsburg, but to cross the river back into Virginia and put an end to his invasion plans. Lee ordered McLaws to abandon the siege of Harpers Ferry, march northwest along the Potomac and find his way back into Virginia as best he could.

When Lee decided all of this, he had not yet heard from Stonewall Jackson. Later that night, Lee would reconsider his plans to retreat, after receiving some encouraging news — a message from Jackson that told him the day had not been such a disaster after all. By delaying the Federal advance over South Mountain, Lee's troops had given Jackson time to tighten his grip on Harpers Ferry.

On Sunday, while the battles were raging on South Mountain, Jackson had slowly and methodically positioned his artillery around the Federal garrison. Two batteries had to hack a narrow road out of the brush up Maryland Heights to get four Parrott rifles to the summit — a task that required 200 men wrestling the ropes of each gun.

Jackson wanted all the guns to open firing simultaneously. But up on Loudoun Heights, General Walker grew impatient and began the bombardment with his five pieces shortly after 1 p.m. The first shell fell harmlessly on the outskirts of town near where a chaplain was conducting a Sunday service for the 125th New York. Soon the other Confederate batteries joined in. Federal guns boomed in response, but the Confederates on the heights were out of range.

Late in the afternoon, Jackson moved a portion of his troops to a position better suited for fighting the Federals on Bolivar Heights. He had restored A. P. Hill to command after disciplining him for being lax. And Jackson now instructed that fiery soldier to maneuver his infantry and artillery down the west bank of the Shenandoah River in preparation for a flank attack on the Federal left at Bolivar Heights the next morning. By nightfall, Hill controlled a knoll on the southern part of the heights and had two brigades along the Shenandoah to the Federal rear.

The besieged Federals doubted that they could hold out for another 24 hours, as Miles had predicted in his message to McClellan the night before. McClellan had received that message Sunday morning and had replied with an order to Miles to "hold out to the last extremity. If it is possible, reoccupy the Maryland Heights with your whole force. If you can do that, I will certainly be able to relieve you." But the order never got through, though McClellan sent it by three different couriers on three different routes.

Maryland Heights was, in fact, ripe for recapture. Only a single Confederate regiment now occupied the crest, McLaws having taken the remainder north to face the Federals attacking through Crampton's Gap. But Miles did not know this, so nothing was done to retake Maryland Heights. Indeed, Miles appeared so paralyzed that one regimental commander even suggested the unthinkable to his fellow officers: mutiny to remove Miles from command.

Another regimental commander, Colonel Benjamin F. Davis of the 8th New York Cavalry, sought to salvage something from the debacle. He proposed to Miles that the Federal troopers — his own regiment, the 12th Illinois Cavalry, and smaller units of Maryland and Rhode Island cavalry — attempt to break out of the Confederate encirclement. The 1,400 cavalrymen would be useless in defending Harpers Ferry, Davis argued, and a successful breakout would deprive the Confederates of all those good horses.

At first, Miles would not hear of it. The idea, he stormed, was "wild and impractical." But Davis was determined — and he

Captain Wilson Colwell of the 2nd Wisconsin was killed on the evening of September 14 as he led two companies of skirmishers against Alfred Colquitt's brigade at Turner's Gap. Wrote Colwell's commanding officer, "His place can hardly be filled. He was a fine officer and beloved by the whole regiment."

was a man to reckon with. The young colonel was something of a rarity in the U.S. Army; he was a Southerner — Alabama-born and Mississippi-raised — who had remained loyal to the Union. Jeb Stuart had been a classmate of his at West Point, and after they went their separate ways, Davis may have felt a compulsion to match his illustrious foe in audacity. At any rate, he was a fierce and daring commander. When Miles saw that Davis intended to break out, with or without permission, he relented.

After dark, the horsemen began forming up in a column of twos on Shenandoah Street in Harpers Ferry, facing the pontoon bridge that led across the Potomac north into Maryland. The garrison's sutlers, usually a tight-fisted lot, surprised the troopers by handing out free pouches of tobacco. Toward the rear, Major Augustus W. Corliss addressed his 7th Squadron Rhode Island Cavalry, an outfit dubbed the "college cavaliers" because almost all of the members were three-month volunteers from Dartmouth College in New Hampshire and Norwich University in Vermont. Corliss told them that by the next morning they would be free men, prisoners or dead — "in Pennsylvania, on the way to Richmond or in Hell."

About 9 p.m., the column started off at a walk across the pontoon bridge. Benjamin Davis rode at the head of the column along with two guides who knew the country. Breaking into a gallop, they turned left onto a narrow road that wound to the west around the base of Maryland Heights and then north toward Sharpsburg.

Davis fully expected to find Confederate pickets blocking the road at the base of the mountain. But to his astonishment, not a single enemy was in sight.

Even so, the breakout was nearly aborted in the first hour by a wrong turn. After crossing the bridge, Company D of the 12th Illinois turned right instead of left and blundered upon a post of Confederate pickets at the hamlet of Sandy Hook. A hail of bullets sent the errant Federals galloping back to the column.

The moonless night was so dark that the riders could maintain the proper interval only by listening to the rattle of their neighbor's saber and by watching for the sparks of horses' shoes striking the rocky road. Recalled one trooper, "It was a killing pace."

Near Sharpsburg, a dozen miles north of Harpers Ferry, the column narrowly avoided a collision with Confederates who had retreated from Turner's Gap. Quickly Davis backtracked and detoured westward off the road into woods and fields, where the riders threaded their way between sleeping camps of the enemy. The Federals were so exhausted that many nodded off in the saddle.

Just before dawn, the column emerged onto a road leading to Hagerstown nearby. Soon after, they heard the rumbling of wheels off in the distance. It was a wagon train approaching from Hagerstown with Longstreet's reserve supply of ammunition.

Davis concealed his troopers in the woods and boldly rode forward to halt the lead wagon. The predawn darkness blurred the color of his uniform, and his thick Southern accent suggested to the sleepy drivers that he was a Confederate officer. In his deepest drawl, he warned of Federal cavalry ahead, and ordered the drivers to turn right at the next fork.

With Federal cavalrymen leading the way, the unsuspecting drivers obediently turned their wagons onto the road to Greencastle,

This standard was carried by Colonel Benjamin F. Davis' 8th New York Cavalry during its breakout from Harpers Ferry on the night of September 14. The escaping men rode so close to Confederate bivouacs that they could plainly see enemy soldiers silhouetted against campfires.

Pennsylvania, eight miles north of Hagerstown. But there was also an escort of cavalry in the rear — real Confederates. When they rode up to demand why the column was heading north, Davis ordered the 12th Illinois to charge, and the Confederates were driven away. "A change of governments was probably never more quietly or speedily effected," claimed a proud Federal trooper.

Daylight came and the wagon drivers realized that their new escorts were wearing blue, not gray. A driver asked Private Henry Norton the name of his outfit. "The 8th New York," Norton replied with a smile. "The

Hell you say!" exclaimed the startled driver.

A little after 9 a.m. that Monday, the Federals reached Greencastle. Davis brought with him more than 40 enemy ordnance wagons, and he had not lost a single man in combat. He and his men had pulled off the first great cavalry exploit of the War for the Army of the Potomac. "The boys thought soldiering wasn't so bad after all," exulted Private Norton.

The cavalry breakout could not have been more timely. During the night, Jackson sent 10 guns across the Shenandoah to support A. P. Hill's artillery, positioning them near the base of Loudoun Heights so that they could enfilade the rear of the Federal line on Bolivar Heights. Altogether, nearly 50 Confederate guns were ready, and when the mist lifted early Monday, they opened up on Harpers Ferry with such fury, wrote Colonel William H. Trimble of the 60th Ohio, that there was "not a place where you could lay the palm of your hand and say it was safe."

About 8 a.m., as Jackson prepared to launch a full-scale infantry assault, Colonel Miles met with his top officers. Miles pointed out that his batteries were almost out of ammunition and that relief from McClellan no longer appeared imminent. Miles concluded, and his officers reluctantly agreed, that further resistance was useless.

The order to surrender flashed along Bolivar Heights. A cook from the 115th New York cut a piece of canvas from a white tent and tied it to a tree. Other white flags popped up, and the Confederate guns gradually fell silent. Federal Brigadier General Julius White rode forward to negotiate terms of surrender. At least one gun kept firing, however, sending a shell that exploded directly behind Miles and nearly severed his left leg.

As Miles lay mortally wounded (he would die the following day), the humiliation felt by his men at having to surrender gave way to anger. They remembered their grievances against Miles: his failure to defend Maryland Heights adequately, and the fact that he had released Confederate prisoners on parole as recently as the previous day, naïvely trusting them not to divulge details of the Federal defenses. Old Miles had sold them out, many Federals muttered; he was a traitor. Such was the feeling against him that some thought the fatal shell had been fired at Miles deliberately by a Federal gunner.

The Federals surrendered 73 artillery pieces, 13,000 small arms and 12,500 men — the largest capitulation of Federal forces in the entire War. The prisoners would later be paroled upon their oath not to take up arms until a comparable number of enemy prisoners were released.

Stonewall Jackson left the final details of the surrender to A. P. Hill. As Jackson rode down into the town of Harpers Ferry, defeated Federals lined his path to get a look at their famous conqueror. They marveled at his seedy appearance. "Boys, he is not much for looks," remarked Emmery Matlock of the 15th Indiana Battery, "but if he had been in command of us we would not have been caught in this trap."

The Confederates had little time to savor their victory. There were urgent new marching orders from Robert E. Lee. All the wings of the army were to reunite as soon as possible at Sharpsburg.

All that night, Jackson's grimy columns moved out along the Charleston Turnpike toward Sharpsburg. Captain Edward Ripley of the 9th Vermont, exhausted by the tension of the siege and humiliated by the Federal surrender, watched in amazement. "It was a weird, uncanny sight," he wrote, "and drove sleep from my eyes. They were silent as ghosts; ruthless and rushing in their speed; ragged, earth-colored, dishevelled and devilish, as though keen on the scent of hot blood. Their sliding dog-trot was as though on snow-shoes. The shuffle of their badly shod feet on the hard surface of the Pike was so rapid as to be continuous like the hiss of a great serpent. The spectral picture will never be effaced from my memory."

The Push to Dunker Church

*"No tongue can tell, no mind conceive, no pen portray the horrible sights
I witnessed this morning."*

CAPTAIN JOHN TAGGERT, 9TH PENNSYLVANIA RESERVES, SEPTEMBER 17, 1862

3

On Monday morning, September 15, the Confederates retreating west from South Mountain crossed a meandering watercourse called Antietam Creek and approached the little Maryland town of Sharpsburg. As the weary, footsore columns climbed a gradual slope leading from the creek, Robert E. Lee gestured to an undulating ridge beyond which lay the town and announced: "We will make our stand on those hills."

That noon, further news from Harpers Ferry strengthened Lee's resolve to fight the Federals at Sharpsburg. A courier from Jackson came galloping up to report the surrender of the Federal garrison. "That is indeed good news," said Lee. "Let it be announced to the troops."

Yet until Jackson arrived from Harpers Ferry, 12 miles to the south, Lee would have to make do with a dangerously weak force: Longstreet's two divisions and D. H. Hill's battle-depleted division. These totaled no more than 18,000 men, less than one third the number of pursuing Federals. When one of Lee's artillery officers expressed concern about the prospect of facing the Federals, Lee confidently reassured him that McClellan would not attack on that day, nor even on the morrow.

The ground Lee chose for battle promised strong defensive positions, though hardly impregnable ones. Its most prominent feature was the tree-lined Antietam, which flowed in a north-south course less than a mile east of Sharpsburg before joining the

Potomac three miles south of the town. The creek itself constituted only a minor barrier. Ranging from 60 to 100 feet in width, it was fordable in places and crossed in the immediate vicinity by three stone bridges, each a mile or so apart.

West of the creek, the terrain was more formidable. North of Sharpsburg, the ridge that Lee had pointed out to his troops ran roughly parallel to the course of the Antietam a mile or so away. And the ground up the slope was mostly open, consisting of neatly fenced cornfields and pastures; only an occasional patch of woods interrupted a clear field of fire. South of Sharpsburg, steep bluffs commanded the lower crossings of the Antietam.

Lee deployed his troops along the ridge in a line about four miles long. At its extreme northern end the line bent westward to anchor on a loop in the Potomac. To the south it jutted eastward to follow the bluffs overlooking the creek.

The terrain provided excellent cover for Lee's infantrymen: rail and stone fences, waist-high outcroppings of limestone, little hollows and swales. Northeast of town there was even an old sunken road, so deeply worn down by wagon wheels that it offered a kind of natural trench.

Although the Confederate line would be stretched thin, even after Jackson's arrival, another geographical feature would be of help to the defenders. Just west of the ridge ran a major north-south road, the

Troops of Major General Joseph Hooker's I Corps cross Antietam Creek at a ford above Sharpsburg on September 16, 1862. The following dawn, I Corps spearheaded the Federal attack on the Confederate left.

turnpike connecting Hagerstown, Sharpsburg and Harpers Ferry; this promised to be a perfect route for shifting troops back and forth rapidly.

The terrain had one troubling feature for the defenders. They would have to fight with their backs almost to the Potomac. The narrow strip of land between Sharpsburg and the river left little room for maneuver if they were forced to fall back. And in this looping length of the Potomac, there was only one crossing place: Boteler's Ford, near the village of Shepherdstown, where Jackson was expected on Tuesday. If the defenders were squeezed back into this bottleneck, they would face annihilation from Federal artillery. This risk alone would have caused virtually any general but Lee to retreat. But above all else Lee was a warrior. As a Confederate officer later concluded: "I do not think General Lee wanted to leave Maryland without a fight."

Lee would have his fight — "a great enormous battle," as a Wisconsin officer would describe it, "a great tumbling together of all heaven and earth."

As Lee had predicted, the cautious McClellan pursued slowly. The first two Federal divisions appeared east of the Antietam on the afternoon of Monday, September 15, but it was dark before the bulk of the Army of the Potomac reached the vicinity.

McClellan, riding up late that afternoon, was in high spirits. He had failed to save Harpers Ferry, but at South Mountain he had won what he described in a letter to his wife as a "glorious victory." And if the day's telegram from Washington was any indication, he was back in the good graces of President Lincoln, who wired: "God bless you and all with you. Destroy the rebel army if possible."

Now, with the Confederates vastly out-

numbered and pushed up against the Potomac, McClellan had a splendid chance to make good his vow to "whip Bobbie Lee." McClellan personally reconnoitered the Confederate line from the hills east of the Antietam, coming under the fire of an enemy battery. He also tended to the details of getting up his supply trains and putting every division in position. The Federals, however, were deploying at a snail's pace. "Nobody seemed to be in a hurry," observed one of McClellan's aides, Lieutenant James H. Wilson. "Corps and divisions moved as languidly to the places assigned them as if they were getting ready for a grand review instead of a decisive battle."

Except for occasional artillery exchanges, the most exciting event on Tuesday morning was a bit of Federal tomfoolery. A pair of young daredevils from the staff of Brigadier General Thomas Meagher's Irish Brigade challenged each other to a cross-country race on horseback. One contestant was a surgeon by the name of Francis Reynolds; the other was Captain Jack Gosson, a free spirit who had learned his horsemanship in the Austrian Hussars.

Gosson and Reynolds went galloping off. They raced from field to field, jumping fences and ditches as if competing in a peacetime steeplechase. Soon, to the cheers of their comrades, they dashed out beyond the Federal skirmish line, ignoring orders to halt, and rode within easy rifle range of the enemy. But instead of shooting, the Confederate pickets shouted their approval and tossed their hats into the air.

As the Federals whiled away the day, three of Stonewall Jackson's divisions began arriving in Sharpsburg after marching all night from Harpers Ferry. The arrival of these troops reduced the numerical odds against the Confederates to about 2 to 1. Reporting to General Lee, John Walker was surprised to find his chief looking "calm, dignified, and even cheerful. If he had had a well-equipped army of a hundred thousand veterans at his back, he could not have appeared more composed and confident."

Once again, McClellan's caution and insistence on attending to every detail had cost him the opportunity to strike at the enemy when he was most vulnerable. It was not until 2 p.m. on Tuesday — nearly 24 hours after McClellan reached the Antietam — that he completed his plan of battle and began issuing orders for an attack at dawn on Wednesday.

"The design," he reported later, "was to make the main attack on the enemy's left." This intention was dictated largely by the Confederate defenses at the three bridges spanning the Antietam. The lower bridge, a mile southeast of Sharpsburg, was directly beneath strong Confederate positions on the bluffs overlooking the Antietam. The middle bridge, on the road from Boonsboro, was subject to Confederate artillery fire from the heights near Sharpsburg. The upper bridge, however, lay two miles east of the Confederate guns and thus safely out of range. Here, on the northern flank, McClellan planned to commit more than half of his army. Two corps would initiate the assault, supported by a third and, if necessary, a fourth.

Along with this major effort against the enemy left, McClellan intended to launch a diversionary attack against the Confederate right with a separate corps. If either attack succeeded, McClellan planned to strike the center with any available reserves.

In deploying his troops to fit this design, McClellan dismantled his command structure. Each corps, instead of being subordinated to one of three semi-autonomous wings of the army, would now constitute a separate command responsible to McClellan himself. With the arrival of a second division of Major General Fitz-John Porter's V Corps from Washington, McClellan now had five corps in front of the Antietam. One additional corps, William Franklin's VI, was only six or seven miles away in Pleasant Valley, sitting idle after having allowed McLaws' Confederates to withdraw unmolested.

The new command structure placed a heavy burden on McClellan. Once the attack began, he would have to coordinate the actions of six separate corps commanders. Unless he maintained a tight grip, his battle plan could easily degenerate into a series of disconnected engagements.

McClellan did little to help himself. In informing subordinates of his plans for the battle, he issued to each commander only orders for his own corps, not general orders that would spell out the role of each corps in the overall scheme. The terrain would make coordination even more difficult. The rugged terrain, laced with small ravines and hollows, would blind men to what was happening only a few hundred yards to the left or right.

To spearhead the attack, McClellan selected Joseph Hooker's I Corps. The 47-year-old Hooker was a tall, handsome, florid-faced general who insisted on riding a big white horse even though, as one of McClellan's aides remarked, the showy steed "made him a most conspicuous mark for enemy sharpshooters." Referred to as "Fighting Joe" in newspaper accounts, Hooker pro-fessed not to like the nickname, saying it made him sound like a bandit. But it neatly described his conduct. He drank hard, talked tough and fought courageously. He was also vain and transparently ambitious. There was talk that he was the one who had prevailed upon McClellan to change the command structure on the eve of the attack — to escape from under the command of Ambrose Burnside and increase his own authority.

About 4 p.m. on Tuesday, Hooker set his three divisions in motion. They crossed the Antietam at the upper bridge and at nearby fords around Samuel Pry's gristmill and marched west toward the Confederate left flank. Their goal was merely to get in position for the following morning's attack, but some of the columns passed close to a large grove of trees on the left. There, hidden in what military maps would later label as the East Woods, were enemy skirmishers from John B. Hood's division.

As the sun set, a sharp fire fight erupted. Artillery from both sides unlimbered, and the woods and fields resounded with the shriek of shells. A case shot burst in front of the 10th Pennsylvania Reserves and sent lethal shrapnel through the ranks. One of the Federals felt the sudden impact and sensed with horror what seemed to be blood running down his legs. Helped back to the surgeon, he discovered with relief that it was water trickling down; only his canteen had been pierced.

Hardest hit were the 13th Pennsylvania Reserves, the "Bucktails," so named for the deer tails that they wore in their caps. Before darkness ended the fighting, they lost 20 wounded and five killed, including their capable commander, Colonel Hugh McNeil.

Colonel Hugh W. McNeil, commander of the 13th Pennsylvania Reserves, was the first Federal officer to die at Antietam. A Yale-educated scholar and former law partner of William Seward, Lincoln's Secretary of State, McNeil was shot during a skirmish on the eve of the battle.

preparations. Sensing that Hooker's move had signaled the main Federal thrust, Robert E. Lee, from his headquarters tent on a knoll west of Sharpsburg, ordered his left flank to pivot north to meet it. Lee also sent off urgent pleas to two commanders who had yet to arrive from the south: Lafayette McLaws with two divisions and A. P. Hill with one division.

Three miles east of Lee's headquarters, McClellan was also making last-minute adjustments. Shortly before midnight from his headquarters on the lawn of the Philip Pry house, 250 yards east of the Antietam, he ordered XII Corps, under Major General Joseph Mansfield, to move across the upper bridge to back up Hooker. Major General Edwin Sumner's II Corps, also in support, was to be ready to cross the Antietam before dawn. Off to the south, General Franklin received a message to march at daybreak, bringing two divisions of his VI Corps to the Antietam and leaving the division of Major General Darius Couch to take control of Maryland Heights overlooking Harpers Ferry.

Having moved their pieces around the board, McClellan and Lee awaited the morrow. McClellan had more than 70,000 fighting men at hand. With the arrival of McLaws and A. P. Hill, Lee would have about 40,000 — only a third of the total that McClellan imagined he had. The Federals had superiority in artillery as well: approximately 300 guns to the Confederates' 200. But the Confederate batteries held the more favorable ground.

Local residents made hasty preparations to protect themselves. Many of Sharpsburg's 1,300 inhabitants took refuge in their cellars, but at least 200 sought shelter in a large cave

Meanwhile, most of I Corps reached its destination near the Hagerstown Turnpike and bivouacked behind a ridge on a farm owned by one Joseph Poffenberger. Several of the newspaper correspondents Hooker liked to cultivate camped with his corps that night, and as the firing from the East Woods died out, a reporter from *The New York Times* heard Hooker declare, "We are through for tonight, but tomorrow we fight the battle that will decide the fate of the Republic."

About 9 p.m. it began to rain. But neither drizzle nor darkness put an end to the near the Potomac. Before leaving, the farmers over whose ground the battle would rage tried to safeguard their livestock. Near the East Woods, Samuel Poffenberger hid his prize horses in the cellar and muffled their hoofs in feed sacks so that the soldiers would not hear them stomping about.

Not many men slept well. The rain soaked and chilled them. Sergeant William Harries of the 2nd Wisconsin felt as if "a chunk of ice had been drawn up and down my back." Nerves grew taut with every noise. Jumpy pickets on both sides punctuated the night with bursts of gunfire. Near the lower bridge, a soldier from the 103rd New York nearly set off panic in the Federal line when he stumbled over the regiment's dog and noisily knocked over a stack of muskets.

Even the animals seemed to feel the tension. Behind the Confederate line, a group of cavalry horses stirred uneasily. "Suddenly something seemed to pass through the animals like a quiver of motion," an officer on Longstreet's staff recalled. Then the horses broke their picket ropes and stampeded, nearly trampling the cavalrymen trying to sleep nearby.

An hour before sunrise, General Hooker rose from his bed in Joseph Poffenberger's barn. Impatient for the battle to begin, he rode south through a patch of trees — later designated the North Woods — and reached the edge of his picket line. As the first light streaked the sky, he peered south down the Hagerstown pike.

The rain had stopped, but ground fog hugged the hollows; through the mist Hooker could make out his morning's objective. About a mile away, near the point where a country lane called the Smoketown Road joined the pike, the ground rose in a slight

plateau. Hooker wanted this little patch of high ground.

To the west, just across the pike from the plateau, was a landmark by which Hooker could guide his advance: a one-story whitewashed brick building that stood out sharply against the green backdrop of woods. Many of the Federals that morning would mistake it for a schoolhouse, but the building in fact was the house of worship for a congregation of the German Baptist Brethren. The locals referred to it as the Dunker Church because the congregation believed in baptism by total immersion. The members were unpretentious folk who wore simple black hats and bonnets and forsook such vanities as church steeples.

The Dunker Church marked the southern boundary of the field on which the early-morning combat would be waged (*map, page 69*). The battlefield formed a rough rectangle

Alarmed by the two great armies gathering near their town, citizens of Sharpsburg flee southward along the Hagerstown pike on the day before the battle. A number took refuge in caves along the Potomac River.

about a mile long and a half mile wide. To the west was an L-shaped grove of hickory and oak. These West Woods jutted back from the pike just north of the church, then turned north for several hundred yards to a point about halfway between the church and the place where Hooker stood studying the terrain. Just a half mile to the east of this grove stood the East Woods, where Hooker's men had encountered Hood's Confederates the previous evening.

The ground between these two belts of wood consisted mostly of open pasture on the farm of David R. Miller. But in the middle, along the eastern edge of the Hagerstown pike, was a 20-acre field of ripe corn, whose stalks stood higher than a man's head. There were other fields of corn in the general area, but hereafter this one would be called the Cornfield.

Though Hooker could not see his enemy

through the mist, the southern half of this rectangle teemed with Stonewall Jackson's three divisions. Jackson's main line of defense faced north on an east-west axis, crossing the pike about 300 yards north of the Dunker Church. On the Confederate left, Jackson's old division, now under Brigadier General John R. Jones, occupied the northern jog of the West Woods and the open field between the woods and the pike. Hood's division, detached from Longstreet, was in reserve behind the Dunker Church. On Jackson's right, the division of Brigadier General Alexander Lawton extended from the pike through a pasture south of the Cornfield; then it bent southward to skirt the edge of the East Woods, crossed the Smoketown Road onto the Samuel Mumma farm and hooked up with D. H. Hill's division and the rest of Lee's defense line, which ran roughly north-south and faced east.

Jackson had 7,700 men — 1,000 or so fewer than Hooker. This numerical disparity was easily offset by the Confederates' strong defensive position behind ridges, trees, limestone ledges and piles of fence rails.

Hooker launched his advance about 5:30 a.m. His three divisions pushed south, covering a front a half mile wide. Abner Doubleday's division, moving through the North Woods near the Hagerstown pike, constituted the Federal right. Most of George Meade's Pennsylvania division deployed in the center and slightly to the rear. On the Federal left, Brigadier General James Ricketts' division, with one of Meade's brigades in front as skirmishers, descended upon the East Woods.

As Doubleday's columns emerged from the North Woods and the sun appeared over

South Mountain, Confederate guns opened fire. Their aim was so accurate that the second shell burst in the ranks of the 6th Wisconsin, killing two men and wounding 11.

That shell opened a duel of cannon described by one Confederate as "artillery hell." The shell was fired from a knoll on the farm of Jacob Nicodemus, about a half mile west of the pike. There Jeb Stuart had assembled eight cannon from his own horse artillery and a dozen of Jackson's guns. Almost immediately, these guns were joined in firing by four batteries from Colonel Stephen D. Lee's artillery battalion deployed on the high ground across the pike from the Dunker Church.

Federal artillery roared back. Hooker's nine batteries opened up from the ridge on Joseph Poffenberger's farm behind the North Woods. Then the Federals' big guns, four batteries of 20-pounder Parrott rifles, began to blaze away from the hills two miles east of Antietam Creek. A reporter from New York pulled out his watch and calculated that the 24 Parrotts were firing, in aggregate, about 60 rounds a minute — a shot every second.

"Each discharge was at first discernable," wrote Colonel Adoniram Judson Warner of the 10th Pennsylvania Reserves, "but after a little grew so rapid from all the guns brought into play from both sides that it became one prolonged roar."

Advancing on the Federal left under this canopy of arching shells, Brigadier General Truman Seymour's five Pennsylvania regiments drove all the way to the southern edge of the East Woods at the Smoketown Road. There they ran into the far right of the Confederate line, a section manned by the brigade of Colonel James A. Walker. Ten years

before, Walker had challenged Stonewall Jackson to a duel. Then a student at the Virginia Military Institute, Walker was enraged because Jackson, his professor, had accused him of talking in class, an incident that led to Walker's expulsion. The duel was never fought, and Jackson now held his unruly former student in high regard.

Soon Walker would be forced to leave the

Major General Joseph Hooker, commander of the Federal I Corps, chafed mightily at the constraints of higher authority. "I don't think Hooker ever liked any man under whom he was serving," a subordinate remarked. "He always thought that full credit was not given him for his fighting qualities."

At dawn on September 17, Lee occupied a line between Sharpsburg and Antietam Creek. Jackson held the left flank and Longstreet the center. Lee left the right flank, the area between the town and the lower bridge, lightly defended in anticipation of A. P. Hill's arrival. McClellan's plan of attack called for Hooker and Joseph Mansfield to hit the Confederate left while Burnside advanced on the enemy's right.

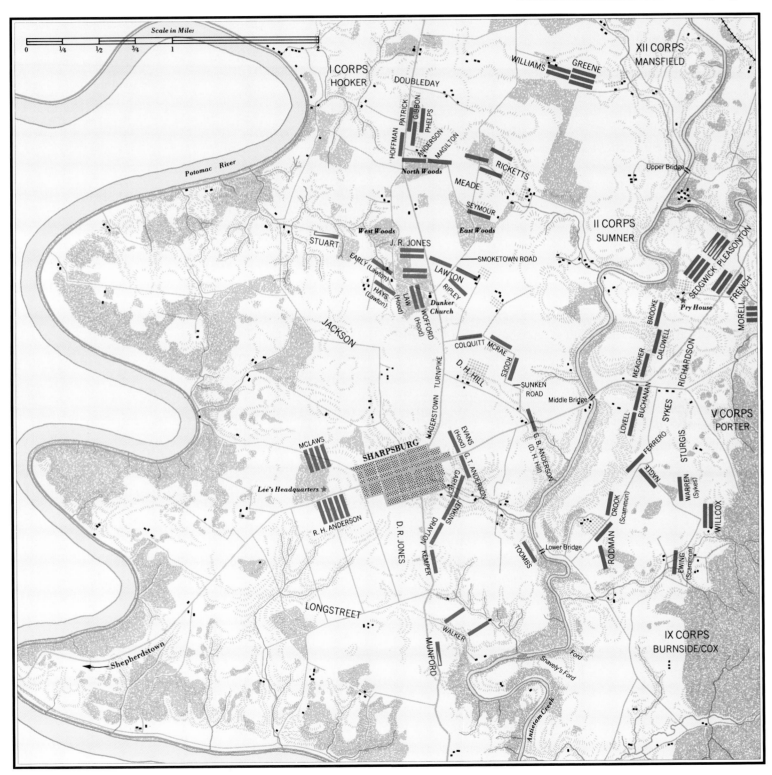

69

field with wounds, but his men put up such a fight that the Pennsylvanians had to pull back through the woods.

All across the bow-shaped front, the Federals were facing stiff resistance. To direct the advance, Hooker rode forward near Miller's farmhouse, just east of the Hagerstown pike. From there he caught a glimpse of the sun glinting off the bayonets of Confederate troops hiding in the Cornfield up ahead. Hooker halted his infantry and brought up four batteries of artillery. These cannon, firing over the heads of the Federal infantry, smothered the Cornfield with shell and canister. The barrage was instantly effective, Hooker noted. "In the time I am writing," he remarked in his official report, "every stalk of corn in the northern and greater part of the field was cut as closely as could have been done with a knife, and the slain lay in rows precisely as they had stood in their ranks a few moments before."

Hooker then looked about for an aide to dispatch for reinforcements. He spotted George Smalley, a reporter for the New York *Tribune* who twice that day would have his horse shot from under him. Hooker pressed Smalley into service as a courier, sending him with verbal orders to a Federal colonel. Once Smalley reached his destination, the officer took one look at his civilian garb and refused to accept his authority.

"Very good," said Smalley, "I will report to General Hooker that you decline to obey."

"Oh, for God's sake don't do that!" responded the colonel. "The Rebels are too many for us, but I had rather face them than Hooker."

The colonel's regiment moved forward, and the entire Federal line pushed ahead. On the Federal left, Ricketts' 1st Brigade, under Brigadier General Abram Duryée, came out of the East Woods and advanced through the Cornfield. Stepping over the bodies of Confederates killed by the artillery barrage, Duryée's four regiments emerged from the stalks into the face of a blistering volley from a brigade of Georgians commanded by Colonel Marcellus Douglass.

Scarcely 200 yards apart, the opposing lines began to hammer at each other. Amid the fury, Isaac Hall of the 97th New York noted with astonishment that his comrades seemed unflustered and "talked coolly of the progress of the battle" even as they loaded and fired.

In line near Hall were two brothers from Lewis County, New York — German immigrants named Gleasman. Suddenly a Confederate marksman, steadying his musket against a tree, picked off one of the brothers. "There is the man who killed my brother," the other Gleasman remarked calmly in Hall's hearing, "and he is taking aim now against that tree." Having spoken, he too went down, a victim of the same marksman.

Presently, the two opposing brigades got help. Three regiments from Walker's brigade on the Confederate right moved west across the Smoketown Road to reinforce the Georgians. One of Meade's brigades in the East Woods came to the aid of Duryée's men. Then the two reinforced lines went at it for 30 minutes or so. "They stood and shot one another," wrote Hall, "till the lines melted away like wax."

More fresh units came up. Then, about 6:45 a.m., Walker's brigade pulled back, having lost 228 of its 700 men. Colonel Douglass' Georgians stayed put despite a 50 per cent casualty rate. Five out of six regimental commanders were shot down, as

was Douglass, who perished on the field.

At the last possible moment, the Georgians were reinforced by the Louisiana Brigade — nicknamed the Tigers — five regiments of Creoles, Irishmen and other groups largely recruited from New Orleans.

The Tigers charged, driving the Federals back through the Cornfield toward the East Woods. The brunt of their attack was taken by the 12th Massachusetts. One of the men, Captain Benjamin F. Cook, described the Tiger attack as "the most deadly fire of the war. Rifles are shot to pieces in the hands of the soldiers, canteens and haversacks are riddled with bullets, the dead and wounded go down in scores."

To counter the Tigers' thrust, the Federals brought up a battery of three-inch ordnance rifles and rolled the guns directly into the Cornfield. The range was point-blank, and the brave Tigers went down in droves.

At 7 a.m., the last brigade of Ricketts' division came into line. This unit had been delayed because, just as the men entered the East Woods and came under artillery fire, their commander, Colonel William A. Christian, broke under the strain. He dismounted and scurried to the rear, ducking and dodging pitifully and muttering about the horror of cannon shells. The unfortunate colonel would resign his commission two days after the battle.

Christian's failure, however, stood in sharp contrast to the courage displayed by the brigade's rank and file as they entered the fray that morning. One of the men, 17-year-old Private William Paul of the 90th Pennsylvania, gathered a detachment of 10 comrades and charged out to retrieve the regimental flag when the color-bearer went down. "A rebel detachment immediately rushed for-

Launching the initial assault of the battle, Federal troops from I Corps charge with fixed bayonets through the Cornfield, on the northern section of the battlefield. They carry their guns at right shoulder shift to avoid entangling the long weapons in the corn or accidentally stabbing their comrades in the ranks ahead.

ward to capture the fallen colors,'' said Paul. "We clashed with a shock!" In hand-to-hand fighting, seven of the Federals fell, but Paul wrenched the flag from a Confederate and made it back to his line, an action for which he would receive the Medal of Honor.

By 7 a.m., charge and countercharge on the Federal left had taken a terrible toll on both sides. The 12th Massachusetts alone lost 224 of 334 men, the highest proportion of casualties of any Federal regiment that day. The Louisiana Tigers suffered nearly as grievously, losing 323 of 500 men in scarcely 15 minutes of desperate combat.

In and about the East Woods and the eastern acres of the Cornfield, the struggle was locked in stalemate. But a couple of hundred yards to the west, the Federal attack had made impressive progress.

The advance of Doubleday's division along the Hagerstown pike earlier that morning had been spearheaded by the four regiments of Brigadier General John Gibbon's Black Hat Brigade, which went into battle with a new nickname. On Sunday, after the attack against Turner's Gap, General Hooker had likened the Black Hats' strength and tenacity to that of iron, and now men were calling them the Iron Brigade.

Moving south with the pike on their right, advance elements of the Iron Brigade flushed enemy skirmishers from the orchard around Miller's farmhouse. Then, at 6 a.m., about the same time that Abram Duryée's Federals plowed into the corn over on the left, Gibbon's men pushed south through a pasture to the northwestern corner of the Cornfield. There they encountered bullets not only from their front, where Douglass' Georgians had moved forward among the corn rows, but also from across the pike, where two small brigades of General Jones's division occupied the open field north of the elbow in the West Woods.

To protect his right flank, Gibbon sent the 7th Wisconsin and 19th Indiana west across the road. Then he unlimbered a two-gun section of Battery B, 4th U.S. Artillery, in front of some haystacks in Miller's barnyard. The gun crews quickly became targets for Confederate sharpshooters, and in a matter of minutes half of the Federal gunners were killed or wounded.

Gibbon hastily ordered up four more guns of Battery B, and the six brass Napoleons raked the Confederates across the pike with case shot. Under cover of the barrage and reinforced by a brigade sent forward by Doubleday, the 7th Wisconsin and 19th Indiana gained a foothold in the West Woods.

It was now about 6:30 a.m., and in the western portion of the Cornfield, Gibbon's other two regiments, the 2nd and 6th Wisconsin, with the 2nd U.S. Sharpshooters on their left, were also pushing ahead. The 6th Wisconsin's Major Rufus Dawes, taking the place of the regiment's colonel who had been wounded, led his men to a rail fence separating the Cornfield from the pasture to the south. A regiment of Georgians lay waiting in the grass.

All at once, wrote Dawes, "a long line of men in butternut and gray rose up from the ground. Simultaneously, the hostile battle lines opened a tremendous fire upon each other. Men were knocked out of the ranks by dozens. But we jumped over the fence, and pushed on, loading, firing, and shouting as we advanced. There was, on the part of the men, great hysterical excitement, eagerness to go forward, and a reckless disre-

Federal Brigadier General John Gibbon, commander of the crack Iron Brigade, was a hard-bitten professional soldier whom a fellow officer described as "steel cold." To be successful in the field, Gibbon asserted, "an army commander must be as near a despot as the institutions of his country permit."

gard of life, of everything but victory."

The 14th Brooklyn, a Chasseur regiment in red pantaloons, moved up to plug the gaps in Dawes's ragged line. "Now is the pinch," Dawes continued. "Men and officers of New York and Wisconsin are fused into a common mass, in the frantic struggle to shoot fast. Everybody tears cartridges, loads, passes guns, or shoots. Men are falling in their places or running back into the corn. The soldier who is shooting is furious in his energy. The soldier who is shot looks around for help with an imploring agony of death on his face."

The black-hatted troops from Wisconsin and the red-trousered Brooklyn men drove south into the pasture. By 6:45 a.m. they had covered a few hundred yards of open ground, about one third of the distance from the Cornfield to the plateau across from the Dunker Church.

Brigadier General William E. Starke was a rising star in the Army of Northern Virginia when he was fatally wounded in the fight with Gibbon's Iron Brigade. The Confederates carried Starke's body back to Richmond, where he was buried next to his son, who had died of wounds suffered at Seven Pines a few months earlier.

Suddenly a new threat materialized on their right. Out of the West Woods and through the pasture west of the pike rushed two fresh Confederate brigades under Brigadier General William E. Starke. Starke had replaced the division commander, John Jones, who had been stunned by a bursting shell. Starke directed his men to positions behind the rail fence lining the west side of the pike, and from this meager cover, they poured fire into the Federals, only 30 yards away across the road.

To meet this new Confederate threat, Dawes's 6th Wisconsin and the 2nd U.S. Sharpshooters wheeled to face west. They had help: From the West Woods, two regiments of the Iron Brigade fired on the flank and rear of the Confederates at the fence; and from Miller's barnyard to the north, Battery B was showering case and canister on the enemy.

After about 15 minutes, the Confederates, caught in this deadly convergence of fire, withdrew to the woods. General Starke was hit by three musketballs and would die within an hour. His men left a grim tableau of wounded and dead heaped up on the ground and spread-eagled on the fence.

Captain R. P. Jennings of the 23rd Virginia lay at the fence with canister shot in his hip and debated with another wounded Confederate the danger of trying to retreat through the gantlet of fire. The other man insisted that the effort was not worth the risk. "I may as well be killed running as lying still," Jennings retorted. Then, driven as much by fear as by courage, Jennings amazed himself by running "like a deer" to the cover of the woods.

With the Confederates falling back on both sides of the pike, the Federals surged toward the Dunker Church. East of the pike, Major Dawes's 6th Wisconsin swept forward, the men "loading and firing with demoniacal fury," he wrote, "and shouting and laughing hysterically." Dawes was only 200 yards from the bullet-scarred church — and from the cannon-girded high ground that was the Federal goal.

Jackson's Confederates, with a great gap torn in their defenses, teetered near collapse. One third of Jones's division west of the pike had been shot down, and it was now commanded by a colonel. Lawton's three brigades east of the pike were in even worse shape; Lawton himself was wounded, and most of his officers out of action.

At this critical moment, a long gray line filed through a gap in the fence in front of the church, raising the yip-yip-yip of the Rebel yell. It was Jackson's last reserve, the 2,300-man division of John Bell Hood.

Hood had been held in reserve that morning in the woods behind the church because his men were hungry and exhausted. The night before, after the skirmish with the Pennsylvania Bucktails in the East Woods, Hood had asked permission to withdraw his men so that they could rest and cook their first real meal in days. Jackson had agreed, but only if the division would stand ready to help at a moment's notice.

The call came a few minutes before 7 a.m. while the soldiers were still cooking up their hoecakes.

Angry as bears, Hood's hungry troops stormed out of the woods and into the wide gap opened up by Gibbon's Iron Brigade. The Confederates' first volley, recalled Rufus Dawes, was "like a scythe running through our line." Taken by surprise, the 6th Wisconsin and the other Federals fell back through the Cornfield. Some stopped and fired as they retreated. But most raced headlong, tripping and stumbling over the bodies of men in blue and gray who already had died vying for possession of that ravaged 20-acre field.

Dawes stopped north of the Cornfield and waved the regimental colors to stem the flight. The 6th Wisconsin was sadly depleted, having already lost 152 of 314 men dead or wounded. Their fallen marked the farthest point of the Federal advance.

As they attacked, the men of Hood's division fanned out to the northeast. Hood's left wing, the famous Texas Brigade, under Colonel William Wofford, advanced toward the western part of the Cornfield; his right brigade, under Colonel Evander Law, headed for the eastern reaches of the Cornfield and for the East Woods.

Hood himself was in the pasture, deploying his troops and guiding his horse carefully for fear it would trample "some wounded fellow-soldier lying helpless on the ground," when one of Jackson's aides, Captain Alexander "Sandie" Pendleton, caught up with him. Stonewall Jackson wanted to check on Hood's progress. Hood replied: "Tell General Jackson unless I get reinforcements I must be forced back, but I am going on while I can!"

Hood's division in fact was not alone. On his right, three brigades of D. H. Hill's division were coming up from the Mumma farm. On the far left, Lawton's remaining brigade, under Brigadier General Jubal Early, was pushing through the West Woods from the Nicodemus farm, where the troops had been supporting Stuart's horse artillery. And a dozen or so of the Confederate guns were being shifted south to Hauser's Ridge, just behind the West Woods, to get closer to the action.

But Hood's men would carry the brunt of the attack. On the right, the brigade under Colonel Law drove the Federals still remaining in the Cornfield back into the East Woods. Two fresh brigades of Federals from Meade's division then counterattacked, reaching the stalks, but Law's men met their thrust. The Federals fell back north of the Cornfield, where they were rallied by a boyish private who stood on a knoll waving his hat and yelling, "Rally, boys, rally! Die like men, don't run like dogs!"

Near the pike, the Texas Brigade bore down upon the western edge of the Cornfield under intense fire from the retreating Federals. Three successive color-bearers of the Texas Brigade's Hampton Legion were shot down, before Major J. H. Dingle seized the flag and shouted, "Legion, follow

McClellan's headquarters at the Philip Pry house overlooked the center of the battlefield (*inset*). But the splendid vista did not afford a clear view of the right and left flanks, where the heaviest fighting occurred.

your colors!'' He led the men to the edge of the corn 50 yards from the Federals and there was shot dead.

To the Hampton Legion's right the 1st Texas rammed forward recklessly in pursuit of the Federals, outrunning the rest of the Confederate line by 150 yards. At the fence on the northern edge of the Cornfield, one of Meade's brigades had regrouped and lay waiting on the ground, their rifle barrels resting on the lower fence rails. The Federals held fire until they could see the legs of the Texans beneath the pall of smoke. When the Texans were 30 yards away, the Federals opened up.

At the same time, the Texans were caught in the flank by Federals firing from across the pike. The cross fire staggered Hood's men. No fewer than nine of the regiment's color-bearers went down in swift succession, and the banner was lost. In not much more than 20 minutes, the 226-man 1st Texas suffered 186 killed and wounded—a casualty rate of 82.3 per cent, the highest percentage lost in battle of any regiment during the entire War.

Along the pike near Miller's barnyard, Gibbon's intrepid gunners of Battery B fought desperately to save their guns, supported by survivors of the 6th Wisconsin and other remnants of Gibbon's brigade. The acrid smell of gunpowder filled the air. The smoke was so heavy that the gunners could scarcely see their targets, though the Confederates charged to within 15 yards of the barrels.

One of the guns was out in the road, blasting Hood's men in the Cornfield with canister. The other five pieces faced south where Jubal Early's reinforcements were advancing into the open field from the West

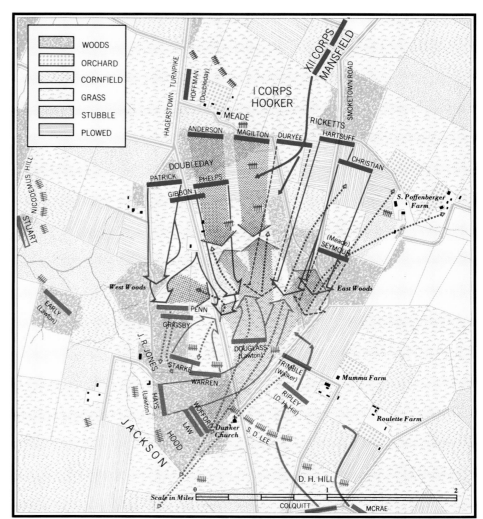

Woods. The battery was loading and firing so rapidly that one gunner forgot to step away when the cannon went off and was gravely injured by the recoil.

As the crewmen fell—40 of the battery's 100 men were killed or wounded that morning—others rushed in to keep the guns working. At one point, General Gibbon galloped up, his face black with powder and smoke. Noticing that the gun in the pike was aimed too high, he jumped off his horse, ran to the gun and adjusted the elevating screw so that the muzzle dropped. "Give 'em hell,

In the early morning fighting, control of the Cornfield seesawed back and forth between Hooker's Federals and Jackson's Confederates. At 5:30 a.m., Duryée's and Seymour's brigades led the Federal advance through the East Woods, followed by the brigades of Christian and George Hartsuff, with Doubleday's division on the right. The Federals met savage resistance from Lawton's and J. R. Jones's Confederates. Then, at 7 a.m., Hood's division counterattacked and hurled the Federals back. Hood's men in turn were stopped by Meade's division at the Cornfield's northern edge. Lines of retreat are indicated by single dashed arrows.

lowed by the remnants of the Iron Brigade.

It was only 7:30 a.m., yet the carnage was monumental. Of Hooker's 9,000-man I Corps, nearly 2,600 had been killed or wounded; that many or more had straggled to the rear or become hopelessly separated from their units.

Hood's counterattack — 30 savage minutes that he later described as "the most terrific clash of arms, by far, that has occurred during the war" — had saved the morning for the Confederates. He had broken Hooker's attack and effectively taken I Corps out of the action. Hood would be promoted to major general because of it, his arrest forgotten.

But Hood's exhausted men could advance no farther, for an entire corps of fresh Federals was coming onto the field. The carnage began anew, and in a matter of minutes, Hood's outnumbered division lost 1,380 men. The survivors, practically down to their last cartridges, were forced to withdraw to the shelter of the West Woods. "Where is your division?" a brother officer inquired. "Dead on the field," replied Hood.

The Federal reinforcements were the 7,200 troops of Joseph Mansfield's XII Corps. Half of the troops moving forward were raw recruits unused to drill and discipline. Mansfield, too, was inexperienced, having taken command only two days before. At the age of 58, he was a veteran of 40 years' service, but most of it had been spent in engineering and staff work. Although brevetted for gallantry during the Mexican War, he had never led large numbers of soldiers into combat.

Worrying that his recruits might break and run if not kept tightly bunched, Mansfield marched his regiments to the front in an

boys!" he shouted, and the gunner pulled the lanyard. The blast blew away a section of fence along the pike — and with it enemy bodies. A Federal officer saw "an arm go 30 feet in the air."

All six guns now switched to double loads of canister. Three times the Confederates mounted full-scale charges in an attempt to capture the battery. Three times the gunners hurled them back.

But after 15 to 20 minutes of frenzied firing, the Federals' ammunition was almost expended. During a lull in the action, Gibbon moved to extricate his beleaguered battery. Though 26 horses lay dead around the battery, he somehow managed to muster enough animals to limber up the guns. Back up the turnpike toward Poffenberger's farm galloped Battery B, soon to be fol-

unwieldy formation known as "column of companies, closed in mass." In this formation, a regiment was arrayed 10 ranks deep instead of two ranks deep as in the conventional line of battle. Vulnerable to enemy fire — presenting "almost as good a target as a barn," noted Captain John Gould of the 10th Maine — the ponderous formation rolled into the East Woods, where the men were confronted with enemy fire.

Time slipped by as Mansfield struggled frantically to deploy his men in line of battle. Just as the 10th Maine became engaged, Mansfield came riding up and ordered the men to cease firing because he thought some of Hooker's men were still in the woods. The Mainers protested, pointing through the woods to the grayclad sharpshooters who had already wounded the regiment's colonel and were even now leveling their rifles. "Yes, yes, you are right," replied Mansfield — and thereupon took a bullet in the chest. It was a mortal wound, and the old general died later that day. Command of the corps fell to Brigadier General Alpheus S. Williams. A onetime judge and postmaster

of Detroit, Williams had proved himself to be an effective commander, popular with his men and steady under fire. With an unlit stub of cigar clenched in his teeth, he got the corps moving forward.

The situation on the field was very nearly the same as when Hooker's I Corps had launched the initial attack two hours earlier. The ground gained by the Federals had been lost. The lines held by the two opposing armies had reverted to the original; only the units were different. Three of D. H. Hill's brigades had come across from the Mumma farm on the Confederate right to support Hood's division. Together with the remnants of the divisions of Lawton and Jones, they controlled the West Woods, the southern end of the Miller farm, including most of the Cornfield, and parts of the East Woods. It was as if nearly two hours of battle had been waged to no other purpose than to litter the field with human wreckage, likened by one Federal to "burnt-out slag."

Soon the din of battle rose again to a mind-numbing pitch. "The roar of the infantry was beyond anything conceivable,"

General Williams wrote later. "If all the stone and brick houses of Broadway should tumble at once, the roar and rattle could hardly be greater."

Williams' Federals battled with the Confederates for control of the Cornfield. This minuscule patch of ground, no more than 250 yards deep and 400 yards wide, presented a hideous spectacle of death and destruction: broken and blood-splattered stalks framing hundreds upon hundreds of shattered men, some of whom lay moaning in agony while the fighting raged over and around them. It was later estimated that the opposing lines surged back and forth across the Cornfield no fewer than 15 times in the course of this awful day.

At the center of the XII Corps line, the 27th Indiana engaged in a brutal fire fight with Georgians and North Carolinians from one of Hill's brigades. Many of the Confederates were firing buck-and-ball cartridges that contained three pieces of buckshot in addition to the standard ball. At close range, these loads sprayed out like shotgun shells. The nature of the ammunition resulted in 11

wounded for every one man killed, but the overall casualty count was enormous. One of the men wounded was Corporal Barton Mitchell, who had discovered Lee's lost order four days previously.

Soon D. H. Hill's two other brigades joined the fight — but these Confederates met with disaster. Samuel Garland's North Carolina brigade, now commanded by Colonel Duncan McRae, moved into the East Woods. Many of the men were still shaken by the death of Garland and by the mauling they had received at Fox's Gap three days before. It was not long before the strain took its toll. As the brigade deployed behind a rock ledge in the East Woods, Captain T. P. Thomson looked to the right and spied a large force of Federals from Brigadier General George Greene's division. "They are flanking us!" he cried in alarm. "See, yonder's a whole brigade!"

The regimental commander tried to quiet Captain Thomson, but the jittery North Carolinians had heard the warning. Panic seized the regiment, then the entire brigade. "In a moment the most unutterable stampede occurred," declared McRae. "The whole line vanished, and a brigade famous for its previous and subsequent conduct, fled in panic from the field."

The sudden retreat from the East Woods left a yawning gap in the Confederate line, and through it swept Greene's Federals. At 61, Greene, a descendant of Revolutionary War hero Nathanael Greene, was among the oldest of the Federal field commanders. But he was also among the most aggressive. He had with him 1,700 men in two brigades, and he took full advantage of the break in the enemy line.

One of his brigades smashed into the Confederate flank at the northeast edge of the Cornfield. The attack, according to Colonel Eugene Powell of the 66th Ohio, left Confederate dead "literally piled upon and across each other." The Confederates were forced back through the corn. But at least one soldier, Private B. H. Witcher, decided to stand his ground. Witcher could see to his left and right grayclad men lying in neat ranks, and he was counting upon them for support. Then a comrade shouted to him that all these men were dead — and to prove it, fired a round into one of them. When the body did not even jerk, Witcher became a believer and joined the retreat.

While the Confederates were being driven back through the corn, Greene's other brigade swung in a wide arc to the left. It emerged from the East Woods onto the Smoketown Road beyond the Confederate right flank. Encountering only scattered survivors of Hood's division, the brigade advanced southwest on both sides of the road. Greene guided the left of his advance by sighting on the enormous pillar of smoke rising from the Mumma farm, where Confeder-

ates had set fire to the house and outbuildings before abandoning the position.

Straight ahead stood the Dunker Church. The 102nd New York was driving toward it so rapidly that Greene had to rein in the regiment while he brought up artillery to provide covering fire. "Halt, 102nd," he shouted: "you are bully boys but don't go any farther!"

Then, with a pair of batteries firing in support, Greene's troops charged, driving Stephen Lee's four Confederate batteries from the high ground east of the Dunker Church. This plateau had been the Federal objective all morning. And now old gray-haired George Greene had his men within reach of the prize.

The Federals were in control of the battlefield east of the pike and had scattered lodgments west of it. There were even some Federals in the West Woods. Those troops, men of the 125th Pennsylvania, had gotten separated from Williams' division. Disoriented, they emerged from the woods a short distance north of the Dunker Church. One company even walked right up to the building and looked inside, but found only enemy wounded slumped on the pews. Elsewhere, however, the West Woods was full of Confederates.

Hooker, attempting to gather the remnants of I Corps for a full-scale assault, rode into the pasture south of the Cornfield. His white horse caught the eye of a Confederate sharpshooter, who sent a bullet through Hooker's right foot. The wounded general was carried to the rear, faint from the pain and loss of blood but thoroughly convinced, he testified later, that his Federals were ready "to drive the rebel army into the Potomac or to destroy it."

In fact, however, the Federal attack had lost its momentum. I Corps was thoroughly scattered. XII Corps, confused and suffering nearly 25 per cent casualties, had spent its drive. With Hooker out of action, there was no Federal general on the field with authority and energy enough to bring together the dispersed units.

On the east rim of the high ground, Greene now faced intense fire from the West Woods. He halted his men 200 yards from the Dunker Church and sent back for ammunition. The firing subsided, and a lull settled over the field where more than 8,000 Americans — Federals and Confederates in almost equal measure — had met death or injury since sunrise. It was 9 a.m. The first phase of the fighting was over, but the ordeal of Antietam had only begun.

Braving a deadly storm of shot and shell, Federal troops from Hooker's I Corps charge toward the Dunker Church (*top right*) during the early-morning fighting.

The caisson at left, abandoned by retreating Confederate artillerymen, marked the approximate apex of Hooker's advance.

Death in a Country Lane

"We were in the very maelstrom of the battle. Men were falling every moment. The horrible noise was incessant and almost deafening. Except that my mind was absorbed in my duties, I do not know how I could have endured the strain."

LIEUTENANT FREDERICK L. HITCHCOCK, 132ND PENNSYLVANIA, AT BLOODY LANE

In the early fighting, Lee had stayed near the front. He had been close enough to the combat to intercept stragglers. One of them had killed a pig and was scurrying to the rear to cook it. The general exploded in a rare burst of fury and ordered the shirker sent to Stonewall Jackson to be shot. Instead, Jackson thrust the man into the thickest fighting in front of the West Woods, where he redeemed himself—as one Confederate officer remarked, "losing his pig but saving his bacon."

On another occasion, Lee was so absorbed in the nearby fighting that he failed to recognize his own powder-blackened son, Robert Jr., a gunner in Jackson's Rockbridge Artillery. Young Bob walked up, saluted and then had to identify himself to his father.

Attuned to the battle, Lee had an almost eerie feel for when to take chances. He had decided to gamble, weakening the right of his defensive line in order to bolster Jackson in the West Woods. From the south Lee sent the division of Brigadier General John Walker and the brigade of Colonel George T. Anderson (known as Tige to differentiate him from the other Andersons in the Confederate Army).

Lee also committed his last reserves, the divisions of Generals Lafayette McLaws and Richard H. Anderson that had arrived from Harpers Ferry shortly after dawn. McLaws joined Walker and Tige Anderson on the march north to the West Woods. Richard Anderson went to the center to support

D. H. Hill's division. All of Lee's reinforcements were reaching the front as the firing died down around 9 a.m.

McClellan, in contrast to Lee, had remained at his headquarters more than a mile east of the fighting. From the yard of Philip Pry's two-story brick house, built on a knoll, he had a view stretching from the West Woods and the Cornfield on the north to the hills south of Sharpsburg.

With McClellan stood his close friend, Major General Fitz-John Porter, commander of V Corps, which was being held in reserve east of the Antietam. The generals had telescopes strapped atop stakes in the ground. Porter peered through one of them, recalled a staff officer, and "studied the field with unremitting attention, scarcely leaving his post during the whole day. His observations he communicated to the commander by nods, signs, or in words so low-toned and brief that the nearest by-standers had but little benefit from them. When not engaged with Porter, McClellan stood in a soldierly attitude intently watching the battle and smoking with the utmost apparent calmness. Everything was as quiet and punctilious as a drawing-room ceremony."

But the telescopes afforded McClellan little firsthand information of the Federals' progress. To make sense of the smoke-shrouded drama unfolding before him, he had to rely upon signal flags and couriers.

Because of his detachment and his innate caution, McClellan responded belatedly to

Color-bearers of the 34th New York display the regimental and the national flags that they carried into battle at Antietam. In the morning fighting in the West Woods, the regiment, whose ranks had already been badly depleted during McClellan's Peninsular Campaign, suffered 154 casualties — nearly half of its strength.

events rather than initiating them. His battle plan was already a shambles. General Burnside had not yet launched his diversionary assault on the Confederate right, and McClellan's design for the main attack on the enemy left had degenerated into a series of disjointed assaults.

His handling of General Sumner's II Corps — assigned to support the Federal right — was questionable as well. Sumner was ready to cross the Antietam an hour before daylight, but had to wait at headquarters, unable to see McClellan, for more than 90 minutes. At 7:20, after Hood's counterat-

tack from the West Woods came into view at the Pry House, Sumner received orders to advance. Even then, McClellan insisted on holding back Major General Israel Richardson's division of II Corps until its place in reserve could be taken by a division from Porter's V Corps.

It would take about 90 minutes for Sumner's troops to march the mile and a half to the battlefield. Sumner was a doughty old cavalryman, at 65 the oldest general serving in the Army of the Potomac. He was anxious to begin, and impatient at McClellan's policy of committing the troops "in driblets," as he put it.

Sumner led his two divisions — under Major General John Sedgwick and Brigadier General William French — rapidly across the Antietam at a waist-deep ford about 2,000 yards east of the Dunker Church, and hurried toward the battleground. Near the East Woods, he paused to deploy his men. He formed the three brigades of Sedgwick's division into three lines of battle, presenting a front about 500 yards wide. His intention was to smash through to the West Woods, turn the enemy's left flank and then wheel south and roll down upon the town of Sharpsburg.

Sumner developed this simple plan with no knowledge of the tactical situation. En route to the East Woods, he crossed paths with General Hooker, but the wounded I Corps commander was being carried to the rear, weak from loss of blood, and they did not confer. General Williams of XII Corps attempted to brief Sumner, but the old man was in too much of a hurry. Williams could have told him that units from I and XII Corps were available to take part in the assault.

Sumner rushed on. He spurred his horse to the front rank of Sedgwick's division and personally led the advance west across the Cornfield. Such was Sumner's haste that he left the East Woods before French's division, trailing to the left, could catch up. When French arrived about 20 minutes later, Sumner and Sedgwick's division were not in sight. French looked off to the south, saw the men of General Greene's division from XII Corps lying at the edge of the plateau across the Hagerstown pike from the church, and veered off southward to the left of them. Without French, Sumner's assault force was reduced to about 5,400 men.

Without looking back, Sumner had led Sedgwick's division across the pike. Cannon shells from Jeb Stuart's artillery on Hauser's Ridge and Nicodemus Heights fell among his troops, but there was no other sign of the enemy. Sumner did not bother to send forward skirmishers, nor did he deploy flankers to the left or right.

Sumner's officers worried about their crowded formations. Less than 50 yards separated the three brigades from one another, leaving little room for maneuver. While the officers admired the old general's drive and courage, they also remembered how he got his nickname. Sumner was dubbed "Bull

Confederates from General Lafayette McLaws' division and Colonel George T. "Tige" Anderson's brigade open up a murderous fire on General Edwin Sumner's advancing Federals in the West Woods in this sketch by artist Alfred R. Waud.

Head" after a musketball glanced off his skull in the Mexican War.

Shortly after 9 a.m., Sumner's lead brigade, under Brigadier General Willis Gorman, crossed the open field west of the pike and 300 yards north of the Dunker Church. Moving at the double-quick, the men plunged into the northern neck of the West Woods. The woods were only about 200 yards deep there, and soon the Federal front line emerged on the edge of a field.

Immediately, Gorman's men came under fire. Stuart's guns opened up on them again, joined by infantry concealed behind the buildings of Alfred Poffenberger's farm 100 yards ahead.

Only a handful of Confederate troops were involved — a few hundred members of Jackson's old division who had survived the earlier fighting. Even so, a lively skirmish

An unidentified private in the 72nd Pennsylvania, a regiment of Philadelphia firemen, stands before a painted backdrop in this *carte de visite*. His regiment, known as Baxter's Fire Zouaves after their colonel, DeWitt C. Baxter, lost 237 men during the surprise Confederate attack in the West Woods.

ensued. While Gorman's front line blazed away at the vastly outnumbered enemy, the division's second and third brigades came up in line into the woods. These Federals in the rear could not shoot for fear of hitting their own front line, but there was no pressing need for their support. Men in the rear stood at rest, leaning on their muskets and talking casually. A few even lit up pipes and cigars.

Then it happened: A murderous torrent of fire erupted against the exposed Federal left.

So sudden and furious was the onslaught, so overwhelming and so uncannily timed, that the Federals who survived swore that they had marched into a carefully planned enemy ambush. In fact, Sumner had unwittingly been on a collision course with Lee's reinforcements.

McLaws' division and Tige Anderson's brigade led the attack, supported by part of John Walker's division. They were joined by Jubal Early, commanding Lawton's division. Early already had his own brigade concealed in a ravine near the southern edge of the woods. All told, the Confederates slightly outnumbered the Federals now in the West Woods.

The first blow fell upon the 34th New York and the 125th Pennsylvania near the Dunker Church. The lines of attacking Confederates slammed into them from the west and south. The impact sent hundreds of Federals fleeing out of the woods and across the pike. In a matter of moments the forest was carpeted with fallen Federals. "Where the line stood the ground was covered in blue," wrote a Georgian, "I could have walked on them without putting my feet on the ground."

When the Confederate firing broke out to

the Federal left, Sumner was on his mount behind Gorman's front line, facing west and directing the volleys against the small force of Confederates on the Poffenberger farm. Suddenly, an officer called his attention to the new force bearing down on his flank. Sumner turned to look and recoiled in disbelief. "My God!" he shouted. "We must get out of this."

Waving his hat frantically, Sumner galloped to the rear to wheel his men left to face the attack. The rear line was the Philadelphia Brigade, led by Brigadier General Oliver O. Howard, who had lost his right arm at the Battle of Fair Oaks three months before. In the few seconds it took Sumner to gallop the 60 yards to Howard, the Philadelphians' left crumbled. Before the Federals could raise their rifles, the Confederates were upon them. In minutes, 545 of Howard's men fell. Howard tried to wheel his line to the left to face the enemy, but the troops panicked. "Quicker than I can write the words," said Howard, "my men faced about and took the back track."

The commanders of the other two Federal brigades were also trying desperately to swing to the left. But with the lines now less than 30 yards apart, the maneuver was impossible. The three brigades, wrote Howard, "were so near together that a rifle bullet would often cross them all and disable five or six men at a time."

Many Federals were afraid to fire for fear of hitting their comrades. A regiment in the middle line lost 60 men without firing a single shot. Another regiment in that line, the 59th New York, fired wildly to the front. Not until Sumner rode up, cursing, did they realize that their bullets were hitting the backs of the 15th Massachusetts.

Brigadier General Jubal A. Early led his own brigade and remnants of Alexander Lawton's division in the attack on the Federals in the West Woods. "Had the enemy gotten possession of this woods," Early later wrote, "the heights which commanded the rear of our whole line would have fallen into his hands."

That unfortunate regiment, taking friendly fire from behind and enemy fire from the front and left, suffered 344 casualties — the greatest numer lost by any regiment in either army that day.

The Federal commanders did their best. Sumner proved to be supremely steady under fire. General Sedgwick, who had turned down an offer from McClellan to command a corps, stuck by his division despite two painful wounds, leaving the field only when a third bullet struck him in the shoulder.

Brigadier General Napoleon Jackson Tecumseh Dana, who was severely wounded while commanding the middle brigade of Sedgwick's division, described the Confederate fire as "the most terrific I ever witnessed." Soon it came from three directions — west, south and east — for the Confederates had worked their way around to the rear. There were also murderous canister charges from the artillery of Jeb Stuart, who had moved his batteries closer to the woods. "In less time than it takes to tell it," wrote Lieutenant Colonel Francis W. Palfrey of the 20th Massachusetts, who was severely injured and captured, "the ground was strewn with the bodies of the dead and wounded."

Palfrey's men were in the middle line, and the only fire they could safely bring to bear upon the enemy was to the rear. There, the rout of Howard's Philadelphia regiments had opened great gaps in the line. At first, Captain Oliver Wendell Holmes Jr., a company commander in the 20th Massachusetts, failed to realize what had happened. When Holmes saw a Massachusetts soldier firing to the rear, he mistakenly thought the man was aiming at Federals and knocked him down with the flat of his sword. Then someone shouted, "The enemy is behind us!"

Holmes himself went down with a bullet through his neck. Lying semiconscious, he heard a voice asking, "You're a Christian, aren't you?" Holmes managed to nod. "Well, then," said the voice, "*that's* all right!" Then the regimental chaplain moved on, leaving for dead this future justice of the U.S. Supreme Court.

Holmes's comrades in the 20th Massachusetts refused to flee. Instead, the men withdrew in good order. In column of fours, with muskets at right shoulder, the troops marched into an open field and formed a new defensive line.

One of the last regiments to leave the woods was the 71st Pennsylvania. Though a part of Howard's Philadelphia Brigade, the 71st had the good fortune to be on the far right of the rear line — separated from the adjoining regiment by some rock ledges. When the Confederates attacked, Colonel Isaac Wistar immediately ordered his men to lie down. Then he had to get them back up to keep them from being trampled by retreating Federals.

Wistar climbed an outcropping of rock to get a better view. He at once became aware of "an appalling state of facts. On our left as far away as the eye could reach all our troops have given way, and the enemy's pursuing lines were already many hundred yards in rear of us with nothing in sight to stop them!"

Wistar decided that it was time to get out and gave his men the order. As his regiment retreated, they were raked by an enemy volley. A bullet hit Wistar in the left shoulder. He had already lost the use of his right arm 11 months before in the Battle of Ball's Bluff. Now, both arms were paralyzed. He fell to the ground, and the Confederates swept over him.

It was 9:45 a.m., about half an hour after "Bull Head" Sumner had brashly led his men into the West Woods, when the last able-bodied Federal got out. After 20 minutes of brutal combat, almost half of Sedgwick's division — 2,255 men — were dead, wounded or missing.

Casualties among the attacking Confederates were slight — until they chased the retreating Federals into the open fields east of the woods. There they ran into a wall of hub-to-hub cannon from I and XII Corps, spewing canister. Now it was McLaws' men who suffered; one half of the 7th South Carolina went down. Altogether, McLaws lost more than a third of the men in his division before the Confederates withdrew into the woods.

Shortly before 10 a.m., Sumner called for reinforcements from Brigadier General George H. Gordon's XII Corps brigade, resting over in the East Woods. Two regiments advanced through the Cornfield but were stopped by Walker's Confederates firing from the West Woods; the Federals halted at the rail fence bordering the pike north of the Dunker Church.

A soldier from the 2nd Massachusetts picked up a Confederate flag from among a heap of dead and dying men. He handed it to a mounted officer, Lieutenant Colonel Wilder Dwight, who galloped up and down the line, flourishing this trophy to the cheers of the men. Minutes later, as the 2nd Massachusetts fired through the fence beside the Hagerstown pike, Dwight was mortally wounded. The pain was so intense that he could not be moved immediately, and when his regiment pulled back toward the East Woods, Dwight was left lying between the lines. There he took from his pocket a letter to his mother he had begun writing earlier that morning, and added a postscript stained in his own blood: "I am wounded so as to be helpless. Good by, if so it must be." He died the next day.

While this fight was taking place, two of General Greene's brigades again came into action a half mile to the south. Out of ammunition and unable to help, Greene's Federals had lain at the edge of the high ground east of the Dunker Church during Sumner's ill-fated foray into the West Woods. Now, issued a fresh supply of cartridges and backed by a six-gun battery, they rose up and repulsed two enemy assaults launched from the vicinity of the church.

The second of these Confederate assaults, carried out by three regiments of Walker's division, cost the 30th Virginia 160 of the 236 men brought into action. Greene's Federals not only drove the enemy back into the woods, but raced after them, pushing about 200 yards into the woods behind the Dunker Church before stopping and calling for reinforcements.

None came. For now, at least, McClellan had no intention of continuing the attack against the Confederate left. In nearly five hours of fighting, six Federal divisions had been committed to the assault, and Stonewall Jackson's defenders still held the line. Jackson was satisfied. "The Federals have done their worst," he remarked to his chief surgeon as he contentedly munched on a peach shortly before 11 a.m.

Though sporadic clashes would continue on the northern flank, McClellan's attention—and the focus of the battle—already had shifted. Furious fighting now raged in the center of the Confederate defenses, about

Captain Oliver Wendell Holmes Jr. of the 20th Massachusetts was shot through the neck as he attempted to maneuver his men into position to meet the Confederate attack in the West Woods. That night, Holmes was found wandering aimlessly about the battlefield by a fellow officer, who cleaned and dressed the wound. Holmes survived and went on to become an associate justice of the U.S. Supreme Court.

Soldiers from the 2nd Massachusetts and the 13th New Jersey, ordered to reinforce General Sumner's beleaguered forces, are cut down by Confederate gunfire at a rail fence bordering the Hagerstown pike. An officer later wrote, "The men were being shot by a foe they could not see."

a half mile southeast of the Dunker Church.

The action on this new front had not been sparked by any design of the Federal commander. Instead, it had developed by accident when Sumner's trailing division, under General French, veered off to the south about 9 a.m. as Sumner's lead division was entering the West Woods. French's intentions were never explained. He may have concluded that General Greene's men east of the Dunker Church were taking part in Sumner's attack and that they required support on the left.

Whatever the object, French's course carried him south past the burning Mumma farmhouse and then southeast onto the farm of William Roulette. Here, inadvertently approaching the center of the Confederate defenses, he encountered a line of enemy skirmishers.

French was a stout, ruddy West Pointer known to his troops as "Old Blink-eye" for his nervous habit of batting his eyes when he talked. Though hardly a tactical genius, he was a fighter. Pleased to find the enemy, French ordered his division forward.

Though only three of his 10 regiments had seen combat, the men advanced zealously. One of them, the 14th Connecticut, chased a group of skirmishers into the farmhouse cellar — where William Roulette and his family had taken refuge — then locked the door on the occupants. Another green regiment, the 132nd Pennsylvania, had to contend with a different enemy: hundreds of thousands of irate honey bees that had been stirred to anger when a shell destroyed their hives in the Roulette apiary.

Shortly after 9:30 a.m., Sumner's son and aide, Samuel, galloped onto the Roulette farm and made contact with the errant division. He told French of the debacle in the West Woods, and relayed an order from General Sumner to draw off the Confederates by attacking the enemy center.

With his three brigades deployed in lines

of battle, French marched south roughly parallel to the Hagerstown pike. South of the Roulette buildings, the ground rose gradually for about 400 yards. Beyond the crest of this ridge, about 100 yards down the hill, waited the main body of the Confederate center.

The center, commanded by General Longstreet, was weakly defended. At the moment, it was manned by D. H. Hill's division of five brigades, three of which had been battered in the fighting on the left earlier that morning. Altogether, Hill could count on perhaps 2,500 men, a force less than half

the size of that advancing against him. But D. H. Hill, who had already had two horses shot from under him that morning, was absolutely fearless.

More important, Hill's two strongest brigades, ably commanded by Robert Rodes and George B. Anderson, occupied a superb defensive position. At the base of the hill lay an old country lane, which separated the Roulette farm from the Henry Piper farm to the south. This lane left the Hagerstown pike a third of a mile south of the Dunker Church, cut east for approximately 500 yards, then bent to the southeast

Captain Joseph M. Knap's Independent Battery E of the Pennsylvania Light Artillery stands in the open field between the East and West Woods where savage fighting raged for five straight hours. During much of the battle, the battery was positioned along the Smoketown Road, adjoining the field.

and zigzagged down to the Boonsboro pike.

The segment of the lane occupied by Hill's men — a part beginning near the pike and extending for about a half mile to the east — was known locally as the Sunken Road. It had been worn down over the years by erosion and by the weight of wagons so that it lay several feet below the bordering fields. This Sunken Road made a perfect rifle trench. After the day was over, it would have a new name — Bloody Lane.

Lying partially hidden in the Sunken Road behind a low breastwork of fence rails, Hill's men waited while French's division

climbed the ridge. Patiently, they watched the troops of the lead brigade mount the crest 100 yards away, pause to dress their lines, then start down the slope.

"There was no artillery at this point upon either side, and not a rifle was discharged," wrote Colonel John B. Gordon, whose 6th Alabama was deployed in the road just to the left of a sharp bend. "The stillness was literally oppressive. As in close order, with the commander still riding in front, this column of Union infantry moved majestically in the charge.

"In a few minutes they were within easy

range of our rifles, and some of my impatient men asked permission to fire. 'Not yet,' I replied, 'Wait for the order.' Soon they were so close that we might have seen the eagles on their buttons; but my brave and eager boys still waited for the order. Now the front rank was within a few rods of where I stood. It would not do to wait another second and with all my lung power I shouted, 'Fire!'

"My rifles flamed and roared in the Federals' faces like a blinding blaze of lightning accompanied by the quick and deadly thunderbolt. The effect was appalling. The entire front line, with few exceptions, went down in the consuming blast. Before his rear lines could recover from the terrific shock, my exultant men were on their feet, devouring them with successive volleys."

On the receiving end was the lead Federal brigade under Brigadier General Max Weber, a 38-year-old German-trained officer and former New York City hotelkeeper. Weber's men, largely German immigrants, had seen only garrison duty. Here, at a distance of no more than 20 yards, they faced well-entrenched veteran troops. For five minutes, the Federals stood bravely. Then they fell back and took cover behind the crest. Weber was shot in the right arm. His brigade suffered an appalling 450 casualties.

A second Federal brigade started over the crest. Commanded by Colonel Dwight Morris, it consisted of three green regiments scarcely a month in service. Silhouetted on the ridge, with their dark blue uniforms and their faces blackened by powder and smoke, they seemed to the waiting Confederates to be eerie apparitions. "Go back there, you black devils!" taunted a Confederate as the defenders opened up once again from the cover of the Sunken Road.

This second Federal advance also faltered, and French had to commit his last brigade — three veteran regiments and one novice regiment — led by Brigadier General Nathan Kimball. Even the veterans were astonished at the sheets of fire coming from the Sunken Road. Private Thomas Galwey of the 8th Ohio was kneeling on the slope when he noticed that "almost every blade of grass is moving. For some time I supposed that this is caused by the merry crickets; and it is not until I have made a remark to that effect to one of our boys near me and notice him laugh, that I know it is the bullets that are falling thickly around us!"

The 132nd Pennsylvania, which had been driven out of formation by the swarm of angry bees back at the Roulette farmhouse, was facing the enemy for the first time. As the regiment marched up the hill, Confederate artillery commenced firing and some of the

Federal troops from Brigadier General George S. Greene's division secure the blazing ruins of Samuel Mumma's farm, located just south of the Smoketown Road. Before retreating from the farm, Confederate Brigadier General Roswell Ripley ordered the buildings burned to prevent Federal sharpshooters from using them as cover.

Pennsylvanians broke to the rear, afflicted with what veterans called "cannon quickstep." Others of the 132nd fought heroically. Lieutenant Frederick L. Hitchcock, the regiment's adjutant, recalled that Private George Coursen sat fully exposed on a boulder, "loading and firing as calmly as though there wasn't a rebel in the country. He said he could see the rebels better there, and refused to leave his vantage-ground."

About this time Hitchcock found himself caught between conscience and duty. Behind him, on the far side of the ridge, the men of the 108th New York lay prone. Their commander, Colonel Oliver H. Palmer, was cowering on the ground with them. General Kimball saw them and ordered Hitchcock to get the New Yorkers moving. But when Hitchcock approached the regiment with this order, he later wrote, the colonel looked up from the ground and "merely turned his face towards me without replying or attempting to obey the order."

Watching at a distance, General Kimball uttered an oath and commanded Hitchcock to repeat the order to Colonel Palmer at gunpoint. If that officer did not obey, the young lieutenant was to shoot him. Hitchcock was

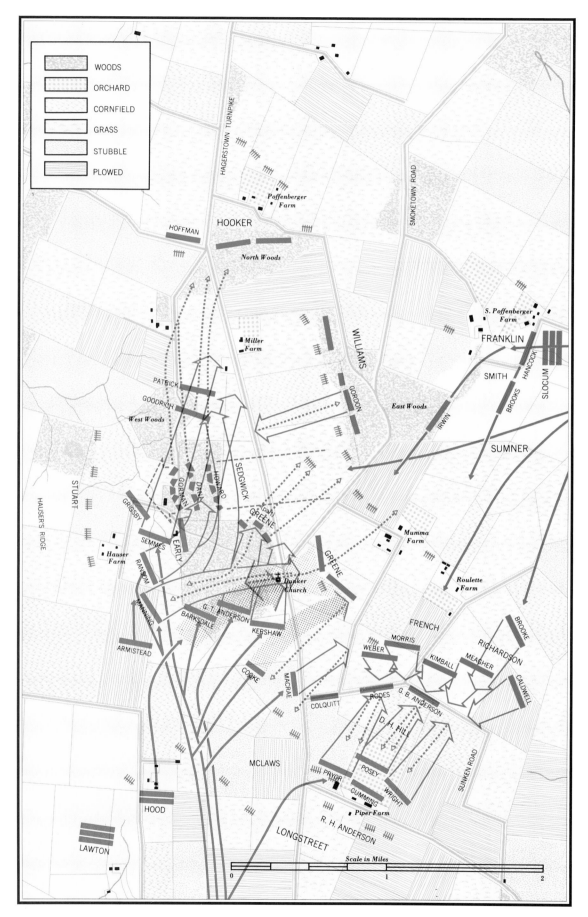

	WOODS
	ORCHARD
	CORNFIELD
	GRASS
	STUBBLE
	PLOWED

HAGERSTOWN TURNPIKE

Poffenberger Farm

HOFFMAN

HOOKER

North Woods

SMOKETOWN ROAD

Miller Farm

WILLIAMS

S. Poffenberger Farm

FRANKLIN

SMITH

PATRICK

GOODRICH

West Woods

GORDON

East Woods

IRWIN

BROOKS

HANCOCK

SLOCUM

SUMNER

STUART

HAUSER'S RIDGE

GRIGSBY

SEMMES

RANSOM

MANNING

ARMISTEAD

GORMAN

DANA

HOWARD

SEDGWICK

GREENE

EARLY

Hauser Farm

Dunker Church

G. T. ANDERSON

BARKSDALE

KERSHAW

COOKE

MACRAE

GREENE

Mumma Farm

Roulette Farm

FRENCH

MORRIS

WEBER

KIMBALL

RICHARDSON

MEAGHER

BROOKE

CALDWELL

RODES

G. B. ANDERSON

COLQUITT

D. H. HILL

MCLAWS

PRYOR

POSEY

WRIGHT

CUMMING

Piper Farm

SUNKEN ROAD

HOOD

R. H. ANDERSON

LAWTON

LONGSTREET

Scale in Miles

0   1   2

Around 9:15 a.m. on September 17, General Sumner led John Sedgwick's division of the Federal II Corps across the Hagerstown pike and into the West Woods, only to be driven back through the Cornfield by Confederates under McLaws, Early and Walker. Meanwhile, another of Sumner's divisions, under William French, veered south of the Roulette farm, sparking a bloody fight along the Sunken Road with Confederates under D. H. Hill.

spared this disagreeable duty by some of Palmer's subordinates, who got the men of the 108th on their feet and led them to the crest of the hill.

It was no use. Line after line of Federals foundered on the long slope. In less than an hour, nearly one third of French's division fell trying to penetrate the enemy defenses in the Sunken Road.

Meanwhile, the Confederates were preparing to mount assaults of their own. Hill's two brigades had been reinforced by Richard Anderson's division of 3,400 men, who came up through Henry Piper's orchard and 25-acre cornfield southwest of the Sunken Road. Many of these fresh Confederates halted in the dubious shelter of the corn and orchard; others crowded into the road, extending Hill's line to the right. Here, on the right, the Confederates made ready to charge out of the road and up the slope in an attempt to flank French's left.

Yet just then, at 10:30 a.m., the Federals were reinforced by Sumner's last division, commanded by Israel Richardson. These 4,000 badly needed troops were the force that McClellan had delayed east of the Antietam until another division replaced them in reserve about 9 a.m.

Richardson led his troops onto French's threatened left. To spearhead a charge, he selected one of the Union's best-known units, the Irish Brigade. Most of this colorful outfit had been recruited in New York early

Under fire from Confederate artillery, Federal troops from Brigadier General William H. French's division close in upon Confederate positions near the Roulette farm during the advance on the Sunken Road.

in the War by the unit's commander, Brigadier General Thomas Francis Meagher, a flamboyant Irish revolutionary who had been interned by the British on the Pacific island of Tasmania and had subsequently escaped. Meagher recruited Irish immigrants who, like himself, envisioned service in the Federal Army as training for a war to free their homeland from English rule.

The Irishmen advanced up the slope to the crest in front of the Sunken Road with their unique panoply and ritual. Emerald flags, embroidered in gold and decorated with shamrocks and Irish harps, snapped in the breeze. Back and forth across their front rode one of the regimental chaplains, Father William Corby, who shouted the words of conditional absolution prescribed by the Roman Catholic Church for those who were about to die.

At the crest, the Irishmen were greeted by a thunderous volley, and the color-bearer of the 69th New York went down, dropping his green flag on the clover-speckled grass. Meagher, in front on his white horse, shouted, "Boys, raise the colors and follow me!" In minutes, seven more men fell bearing the flag. Finally, Captain James McGee retrieved the fallen colors. A Confederate bullet snapped the standard in two, and another ripped through McGee's cap, but he charged on, waving the banner to the cheers of the men.

Meagher's men passed over the crest and moved toward the Sunken Road. From that shelter the Confederates once again leveled a lethal volley. Meagher tumbled off his white horse. The animal had been shot, Meagher would later report, but rumors circulated that he was drunk and had fallen off. In any case, he was badly stunned and was helped to the rear. His men were dropping by the score, and the charge collapsed. The brigade huddled on the slope and fired until, with 540 men dead or wounded and ammunition almost gone, it was ordered to the rear.

The Irish were relieved by another of Israel Richardson's brigades, that under Brigadier General John C. Caldwell. As Caldwell's troops descended into the maelstrom, General Richardson was up front as usual. He was a 46-year-old West Point graduate, a Mexican War hero who had resigned from the U.S. Army in 1855 to take up farming in Michigan. Richardson even looked like a farmer; with his swarthy face and square jaw he would often slouch around camp wearing a battered straw hat and an old shirt.

In combat, however, he lived up to his nickname, "Fighting Dick." As his troops charged downhill toward the Sunken Road, one of Richardson's officers, Lieutenant Thomas Livermore, looked over his right shoulder and spotted "that gallant old fellow advancing on the right of our line, almost alone, afoot and with his bare sword in his hand, and his face was as black as a thundercloud."

Richardson cried out, "Where's General Caldwell?" Someone answered that the brigade commander was hiding in the rear "behind a haystack." Richardson let out a roar, "God damn the field officers!" And then he pushed Caldwell's brigade down the slope to within 30 yards of the road.

It was now about noon, and the Federal pressure along the half-mile Confederate front was beginning to tell on the defenders. Hill's men had been fighting for roughly two hours against French and then Richardson. They had received little help from Richard

Anderson's division of reinforcements. Anderson went down severely wounded early in the fighting, and after that his command disintegrated and ceased to function as a unit.

In the Sunken Road, other key Confederate officers fell. George B. Anderson, commanding Hill's brigade on the far right, took a ball in the foot, an apparently minor wound that eventually proved fatal. Anderson's successor also was mortally wounded. Before long, every single officer of one unfortunate regiment, the 4th North Carolina, would be out of action.

On the left, the best regimental commander in Robert Rodes's brigade — and perhaps the best in the entire Confederate Army — proved to be a magnet for enemy bullets. As he paced back and forth behind his line of battle, Colonel John Gordon of the 6th Alabama received two balls in the right leg, another in the left arm and a fourth in the shoulder. Faint from loss of blood, the 30-year-old Gordon remembered the promise he had made to Lee earlier that morning: "These men are going to stay here, General, till the sun goes down or victory is won!" He

This regimental banner belonged to the 52nd New York Volunteers, the German Rangers, who advanced on the right flank of Israel Richardson's division in the assault on the Sunken Road. As the flag indicates, the regiment also fought in the bloody battles of the Peninsular Campaign.

was about to remind his men of the pledge when a bullet slammed into his face.

"I fell forward and lay unconscious with my face in my cap." Gordon wrote. "I might have been smothered by the blood running into my cap from this last wound but for the act of some Yankee, who had at a previous hour during the battle, shot a hole through the cap, which let the blood out."

With many of their leaders gone and the dead and wounded piling up on the hard clay in the Sunken Road, the Confederates' line began to crack.

The decisive break came in the center through a combination of Confederate error and skillful Federal maneuvering. Here, where the road bent sharply, the lane was not so deep and the defenders were more vulnerable. Federal Colonel Francis C. Barlow, commanding two understrength regiments, the 61st and 64th New York, saw

this and led his men to a little knoll overlooking the bend.

Barlow wore a crumpled black hat and waved a cavalry saber. He always carried the biggest sword he could find in order to whack stragglers into line. Only 27, he was a former New York attorney who had enlisted as a private and risen to colonel in a year's time. He was a natural warrior, one of the most resourceful Federal field officers. It was said that on this morning, tired of seeing his drummers shrink from duty, he had tied them to his sash and led them forward under fire.

When Barlow's 350 men reached the commanding knoll, they poured fire down into the Sunken Road, turning what had been a shelter into a deadly trap. "We were shooting them like sheep in a pen," wrote Sergeant Charles Fuller of the 61st New York. "If a bullet missed the mark at first it was

Federal wounded seek shelter behind the ruins of Samuel Mumma's smoldering farmhouse. On the knoll in the background, Battery A of the 1st Rhode Island Light Artillery duels with Confederate batteries near the Dunker Church.

liable to strike the further bank, angle back, and take them secondarily."

Barlow's position enabled him to enfilade part of the 6th Alabama, which lay just west of the bend in the road. General Rodes decided to wheel part of the regiment to meet the threat. He gave orders to that effect to Lieutenant Colonel James N. Lightfoot, successor to the unconscious Colonel Gordon.

Lightfoot got it wrong. Instead of pulling back his right so that it would face the threatened flank, he ordered the entire regiment to "about face; forward march." Then Lightfoot compounded his error. Major Edwin L. Hobson of the adjoining 5th Alabama, who had overheard the command, asked if the order was intended for the entire brigade. "Yes," replied Lightfoot. His unit and then the others — all five regiments — turned about, climbed out of the Sunken Road and headed for the rear.

Rodes could scarcely believe his eyes when he saw his veteran brigade breaking like raw recruits. When Lightfoot triggered the break, Rodes had been preoccupied with a wounded aide and then with an ugly wound of his own in the thigh. He looked up to see his men, he related, "without visible cause to me, retreating in confusion." Rodes caught up with his men near the Hagerstown pike, but the damage was done.

Barlow's New Yorkers stormed down into the center of the Sunken Road, capturing 300 prisoners. Presently the remaining Confederates gave way, and Federals filled the road. They crowded upon Confederate bodies piled two and three deep, and kneeled upon what one Federal called this "ghastly flooring" to fire at the enemy retreating through Piper's cornfield.

A soldier from the 8th Ohio came upon the limp form of Colonel Charles C. Tew propped up against the northern bank of the road. Tew, commander of the 2nd North Carolina, had been shot through the head, and blood was streaming from the wound. The Federal noticed that Colonel Tew's sword lay across his knees in the grip of both hands. When the soldier attempted to take it as a battle trophy, Tew instinctively summoned the last of his strength and drew the sword toward his body. Then he pitched forward dead.

While the Federals were regrouping in the Sunken Road, their right flank was briefly threatened in the rear by the 27th North Carolina and the 3rd Arkansas, two undermanned regiments commanded by Colonel John R. Cooke. The 29-year-old Harvard-educated Cooke was well connected on both sides of the conflict: His father was a Federal cavalry commander, Brigadier General Philip St. George Cooke; his sister was married to Jeb Stuart.

With one of McLaws' brigades in support on his right, Cooke had marched east from the Dunker Church into a cornfield on the southern end of Samuel Mumma's farm.

Just before Cooke's attack, a little man stepped forward out of the ranks of the 3rd Arkansas. A barber by trade and a fiddler by avocation, he had a request for his captain: "Sir, would it be all right if I kinda give the boys a tune as they move out? I got my fiddle with me."

The captain agreed, and asked for the old mountain square-dance tune, "Granny, Will Your Dog Bite? Hellfire, No!" With the little man in the lead, sawing away on his fiddle, the 3rd Arkansas moved out.

The Confederate attack was doomed from

the start. The Federals brought reserves around from behind the Sunken Road, and in a stand-up fight at less than 200 yards overwhelmed Cooke's two gallant regiments. Cooke was forced to retreat west of the Hagerstown pike, leaving behind more than half of the 675 men he took in. Among the dead lay the little Arkansas fiddler.

At Piper's farm, meanwhile, Longstreet and his lieutenants were trying to patch together a new line of defense to contain the Federal breakthrough at Bloody Lane. It was shortly after noon, and Richardson's Federals — leaving French's men to hold the Sunken Road — were sweeping toward the Hagerstown pike.

Longstreet, clenching a cigar and still wearing a carpet slipper on his sore heel, summoned every cannon in sight. He found a pair of 12-pounder Napoleons of the Washington Light Artillery of New Orleans, and pushed them up into the middle of Piper's apple orchard. From there, 300 yards or so southwest of the Sunken Road, they opened up with canister, cutting through the ranks of the Federals coming through the corn.

When the artillerymen began to fall, Longstreet sent his own staff officers to man

Federal troops drive Confederates out of Piper's cornfield, south of the Sunken Road, in this sketch by newspaper artist Arthur Lumley. Describing the action, Colonel Joseph Barnes of the 29th Massachusetts wrote: "The shouts of our men, and their sudden dash so startled the enemy that their lines wavered, and squads of two and three began leaving the road and running into the corn."

the guns. The general sat on his mount nearby, holding the horses of his officers, calmly directing the fire and — as one artilleryman remembered it — taking an occasional nip from his flask. Longstreet wrote: "That little battery shot harder and faster, as though it realized that it was to hold the thousands of Federals at bay or the battle was lost."

At the same time, D. H. Hill was attempting to rally the remnants of his infantry. Having lost his third horse to a Federal shell, he grabbed a musket and scraped together 200 men willing to follow him. Hill led them forward on foot through Piper's orchard, noting that even "with the immediate prospect of death before them," the men were so hungry they grabbed apples and devoured them on the run.

Hill led his troops to the right in hopes of catching the Federal advance in flank. His men moved rapidly through the corn and came around the Federal left flank near the Sunken Road.

Here the Confederates ran headlong into the 5th New Hampshire, a tough, scrappy outfit that would absorb more battle losses during the course of the War than any other Federal regiment. Much of their zeal for combat was kindled by their swashbuckling commander, Colonel Edward E. Cross, whose previous adventures included buffalo hunting, Indian fighting and service in one of Mexico's several civil wars. Cross's approach to fighting was summed up that morning in a short speech to his troops before the battle: "You have never disgraced your state; I hope you won't this time. If any man runs I want the file closers to shoot him; if they don't, I shall myself."

To meet the Confederate attack, Cross faced his regiment to the left. A single volley repulsed Hill's little band. Hill fell back, then discovered that several of his officers had managed to muster another force of 200 men. The Confederates came on again through the corn. The New Hampshiremen knelt on the dead in Bloody Lane and blazed away. Cross stood erect, a lean, rangy tower of strength with a long reddish beard. A red bandana circled his bald head, and blood from shrapnel wounds streamed down his face, mingling with the black of gunpowder.

"Put on the war paint!" Cross cried out. Taking their cue, his men tore open cartridges and, like Indians on the warpath, smeared their faces with black powder.

"Give 'em the war whoop!" shouted Cross. A bloodcurdling roar went up, and the men sprang forward into the corn. With help from the 81st Pennsylvania, they broke the enemy attack. The theatrics may not have frightened the foe, but it did serve a purpose; as one of the New Hampshiremen explained, "It reanimated us and let him know we were unterrified."

The Confederate flank attack and Hill's own personal charge failed to dent the Federal advance, but these tactics bought time, enabling Longstreet to get 20 cannon in place along the high ground just west of the Hagerstown pike. The guns unleashed such a mighty barrage that the advancing Federal lines wavered, then stopped.

By this time, shortly after 12:30 p.m., some of Richardson's Federals had managed to get as far as Piper's farmhouse, 600 yards south of the Sunken Road and little more than a half mile short of Sharpsburg. But no farther. Richardson's division had lost more than 1,000 men. The gallant Colonel Barlow had gone down, severely wounded by a piece of canister.

COLONEL JOHN B. GORDON

BRIGADIER GENERAL ROBERT E. RODES

MAJOR GENERAL DANIEL HARVEY HILL

BRIGADIER GENERAL ALFRED COLQUITT

MAJOR GENERAL GEORGE B. ANDERSON

Major General D. H. Hill (*center*), who led the last, desperate Confederate defense of the Sunken Road, took up a rifle and fought alongside the troops. Of the Confederate officers in the thick of the fight, only he and Alfred Colquitt went unscathed. Robert Rodes was hit in the thigh, John Gordon was shot five times, and George Anderson was mortally wounded.

Major General Israel Richardson (*center*), whose brigades under John Brook, Thomas Meagher and John Caldwell eventually took the Sunken Road, was mortally wounded in the fighting. Brigadier General Max Weber, one of William French's divisional commanders, suffered a shattered right arm while leading the initial charge.

BRIGADIER GENERAL WILLIAM H. FRENCH

BRIGADIER GENERAL THOMAS MEAGHER

MAJOR GENERAL ISRAEL RICHARDSON

BRIGADIER GENERAL JOHN C. CALDWELL

BRIGADIER GENERAL MAX WEBER

Reluctantly, Richardson ordered his entire division to fall back behind the ridge north of the Sunken Road. He wanted to regroup there and sort out his and French's regiments before renewing the assault. Above all, he wanted to bring up artillery to counter Longstreet's batteries.

Richardson sent back a plea for artillery. But only a handful of guns were readily available. Of the nearly 300 pieces on the battlefield, he received just eight cannon — a section of horse artillery, and Battery K of the 1st U.S. Artillery under Captain William M. Graham.

Graham's Regulars quickly silenced a couple of the Confederate smoothbores 700 yards away. Then, while the Federals dueled with an enemy battery of rifled guns, an extraordinary incident occurred. A civilian drove his carriage up to Battery K, alighted and, to the astonishment of the gun crews, began handing out ham and biscuits. Then this good Samaritan — a nearby resident by the name of Martin Eakle — loaded his carriage with the battery's wounded. He drove them to the rear and returned for a second load despite a bursting shell that wounded one of his horses.

Captain Graham's six Napoleon smoothbores could not reach the longer-range Confederate rifles pounding his battery. He rode back to report the situation to Richardson. The general told Graham to save the Napoleons for the general advance then being prepared. About 1 p.m., while Richardson was talking, spherical case shot exploded nearby, and a fragment sliced into his side. Bleeding severely, Richardson was carried back to McClellan's headquarters at the Pry House, where six weeks later he would die of his injuries.

Richardson's place as division commander would be taken within the hour by another superb leader, Brigadier General Winfield Scott Hancock. But Richardson's removal from the field — like the wounding of Hooker four hours earlier — served to sap the Federal momentum.

Another major thrust against the Confederate center almost certainly would have split Lee's army and probably doomed it. To prevent a breakthrough, Longstreet had his cannon and little else. The struggle around the Sunken Road had cost him nearly 2,600 men against Federal casualties of almost 3,000. His jumbled infantry commands, clinging to the ridges near the Hagerstown pike, contained no organized group larger than a few hundred men. Behind the pike Colonel Cooke's shattered 27th North Carolina had not a single cartridge. The men were reduced to flaunting their flags to create the illusion of strength. "We were already badly whipped," Longstreet later wrote, "and were only holding our ground by sheer force of desperation."

This was the moment for McClellan to seize control of the battle. To crack the center, he had immediately available a powerful reserve of 3,500 cavalry and the 10,300 infantrymen of General Porter's V Corps, who were waiting near the middle bridge, just a mile from the Sunken Road.

To the north, McClellan had the 12,000 fresh troops of Franklin's VI Corps, which had arrived before noon from Pleasant Valley. McClellan had sent Franklin to bolster the defensive lines before the West Woods.

Franklin, who had performed so cautiously at Crampton's Gap three days previously, was now the only top-ranking Federal who wanted to attack. In fact, about 1 p.m. he was preparing to launch a major assault on the West Woods when General Sumner heard about it. Still shaken by his own disaster, Sumner, who was Franklin's senior in age and rank, forbade him to attack. If Franklin was repulsed, Sumner insisted, the entire Federal right flank would be in peril.

At this point, sometime after 1 p.m., McClellan bestirred himself. He sent a message suggesting — not ordering — that Sumner might hold the line while Franklin pressed into the West Woods. When Sumner saw this message, he exploded at the courier: "Go back, young man, and tell General McClellan I have no command!"

McClellan decided to cross the Antietam and talk with the old general himself. As he rode through the lines accompanied by his large staff, the men greeted him with shouts and cheers. McClellan then listened to the arguments of both Sumner and Franklin. Then he deferred to Sumner. McClellan had concluded, as Franklin recalled him saying, that "it would be unsafe to risk anything on the right."

McClellan ordered both generals to "hold their positions." Similar orders were sent to General Hancock, now in command of Richardson's division at the Sunken Road. Porter's corps and the cavalry were to remain in reserve.

There would be no new attack on the right. There would be no new attack on the center. At a time when Lee was gambling everything to win, McClellan was so fearful of losing that he would risk nothing.

Civilian helpers lift a wounded soldier into a Federal wagon while other volunteers assist a field surgeon performing an amputation. The nearly 17,000 wounded at Antietam so overwhelmed local facilities that the surrounding towns became, in the words of a reporter, "one vast hospital."

An Officer's View of the Battle

A survivor of Antietam, Captain James Hope of the 2nd Vermont Volunteers was a landscape artist by profession, and he set out to reconstruct in his sketchbook the vivid scenes of that awful battle. His ultimate goal was ambitious: to translate his sketches into grand historical panoramas that would show generations to come how and where the brave men of both sides had fought and died.

Although he was racked by dysentery and rheumatism in the aftermath of the fighting, Hope retained sharp memories of the terrible details of combat — such as the sight of a Confederate artillerist who had been nearly cut in two by a shell

(*below, right foreground*). In the Sunken Road, where, he noted, "the Confederate dead lay three deep for half a mile," Hope saw a soldier still kneeling in firing position; shot in the brain, the man had died instantly and remained in perfect equilibrium.

Discharged in December 1862 for medical reasons, Hope labored the better part of two decades creating the five paintings shown here. Veterans of the battle praised the accuracy of his work — one old soldier excepted. A former colonel of Hope's regiment declared, "If I were to criticize, I should say there were not enough dead men on the hills."

Confederate gun crews under Colonel Stephen Lee fire on Sedgwick's division as it advances out of the East Woods. The Federal attackers, led by General Sumner, pushed forward to the Dunker Church and the West Woods, at left. There they were flanked and lost half their number to a counterattack.

111

In search of General Sumner, General McClellan and his escorts *(left center)* gallop toward a Federal battery beside the burning Mumma farmhouse at the edge of the East Woods. In the foreground, 1st Delaware skirmishers inch up a hillside, pushing westward, as French's division *(right)* moves southward against Confederates in the Sunken Road.

Advancing over the bodies of Confederates in the Sunken Road, the 7th Maine attacks through the Piper cornfield. The Federals marched into a deadly cross fire delivered by D. H. Hill's division in the orchard in front of them and Roger Pryor's brigade lining the pike to their right.

General Burnside and his staff *(center)* ride up to supervise the crossing of Antietam Creek by the Federal IX Corps at a bridge that would be named for the general. The smoke along the high ground at left is from the guns of Robert Toombs's Georgians. At right, Confederate prisoners are being marched to the rear.

Copyright secured Aug 26, 1889

"Mowed down," in General James Longstreet's words, "like grass before the scythe," Confederate dead lie in heaps in the Sunken Road — known ever after as Bloody Lane.

Standoff at Burnside Bridge

"The day had been a long one, but the evening seemed longer; the sun seemed almost to go backwards, and it appeared as if night would never come."

LIEUTENANT JAMES A. GRAHAM, 27TH NORTH CAROLINA INFANTRY

As the fighting subsided around the Sunken Road, the focus of the battle shifted south to a graceful stone bridge on the Federal left flank. This 125-foot structure, supported by arches, was the southernmost of three bridges that spanned the Antietam. Because it was so near Sharpsburg, it was the only crossing that Lee chose to dispute. Residents called it Rohrbach's Bridge after the family that farmed the land nearby. But henceforth it would bear the name of the Federal commander on the southern flank, Major General Ambrose Burnside.

According to McClellan's original battle plan, Burnside's IX Corps was supposed to cross the bridge as a diversion while Hooker launched the main attack on the northern flank. On the evening of September 16, McClellan had directed Burnside "to form his troops and hold them in readiness to assault the bridge in his front."

By early the next morning, Burnside had moved his four divisions, numbering roughly 11,000 infantrymen and 50 cannon, to the hills overlooking the eastern approaches to the bridge. Then he obeyed the remainder of McClellan's directive, settling down at his headquarters on a knoll a half mile east of the creek to await further orders.

Burnside was in no mood to exercise initiative. Normally a man of jovial demeanor, he was troubled over his relationship with McClellan. Ever since West Point, they had been intimates — "Burn" and "Mac" to each other. In prewar days, after Burnside had resigned from the Army and gone broke trying to manufacture a breech-loading rifle of his own invention, McClellan had bailed him out by giving him a job with the Illinois Central Railroad.

But in the past two days their friendship had soured. Twice McClellan had rebuked his old friend for moving too slowly. Worse, McClellan had abolished the temporary system of wing commands under which Burnside had charge of both Hooker's I Corps and his own IX Corps.

Burnside took the loss of Hooker's corps as a personal affront. He blamed Hooker for being excessively ambitious and McClellan for appeasing Hooker. He professed to consider the change only temporary. Still thinking of himself as a wing commander, he refused to take direct command of IX Corps, preferring merely to relay McClellan's orders to Brigadier General Jacob Cox, who had taken charge of that corps after the death of General Reno at South Mountain. Such sulkiness was uncharacteristic of a general modest enough to have twice turned down President Lincoln's offers to command the Army of the Potomac.

Cox admired Burnside, of whom he would later write without a trace of malice, "He shrank from responsibility with sincere modesty." But Burnside's pique placed Cox in an awkward position. Uncertain of his own authority, Cox offered to step down and return to his old Kanawha Division, but Burnside would have none of it. Thus,

This unidentified member of the 9th New York Zouaves — a regiment in the thick of the fighting at Antietam — wears the outfit characteristic of Zouave units: baggy pantaloons, short jacket, white leggings and tasseled fez. During the battle, his regiment of 600 men lost 45 killed, 176 wounded and 14 missing.

in effect, IX Corps had two commanders.

The uncomfortable situation adversely affected Cox's generalship. A 33-year-old former Ohio State senator who owed his rank in part to Republican political connections, Cox nonetheless had a flair for military command. Yet little of it would be in evidence here.

Both Cox and Burnside knew that marching IX Corps across the 12-foot-wide bridge in the face of an enemy entrenched on the far bank would be a daunting task. Yet neither general made any attempt to reconnoiter the approaches to the bridge. Though the creek was scarcely 50 feet wide and only waist-deep in places, they made no effort to check out a ford located the previous day by McClellan's engineers.

While their troops waited, Cox and Burnside watched the battles in progress elsewhere on the field. From their hilltop headquarters, they had a good view of the successive Federal advances on the northern flank. They could look down, wrote Cox, "between opposing lines, as if they had been the sides of a street."

A little after 9 a.m., the two generals glanced across the creek to their front and saw long lines of enemy soldiers marching northward. These Confederates, Walker's division, would soon collide with Sumner's troops in the West Woods. Lee was stripping his right flank to reinforce Jackson on the left.

The massive Confederate shift north left only a skeletal force on the southern flank. To defend this front, which extended for more than a mile from Sharpsburg to below the bridge, Lee now had only five thin brigades. These units, the bulk of Major General David R. Jones's division, numbered no more than 2,000 men — less than one fifth the strength of IX Corps.

Four of Jones's brigades occupied the highest of the ridges just east and south of Sharpsburg. The other brigade, under Brigadier General Robert Toombs, guarded the west bank of Antietam Creek at the bridge; Toombs's line stretched downstream for 600 yards or so to cover places where the Federals might attempt to ford the creek.

Toombs, a Georgian who had left politics to join the Army, was disenchanted with his superiors, but he remained determined to distinguish himself in some great battle. "The day after such an event," he wrote his wife, "I will retire if I live through it."

Here was his chance. Though his three Georgia regiments, the 2nd, 20th and 50th, were few in number — 550 men facing 11,000 Federals — they possessed an enormous advantage. Rising up just west of the bridge was a steep, wooded bluff nearly 100 feet high. On this slope boulders from an old quarry and a stone wall running parallel with the creek provided excellent cover. There were also towering oak trees in whose branches sharpshooters could hide.

In addition, a little farther downstream the Georgians commanded the Federals' most likely approach to the bridge, the road from Rohrersville. This little road, lined by rail fences on both sides, ran parallel with the creek for a quarter mile only a few yards from the water — within easy musket range of the Georgians on the west bank.

Toombs could also count on 12 artillery pieces on the heights behind him. And other Confederate batteries could bear on the bridge from the high ground just east of Sharpsburg — the plateau that would become known as Cemetery Hill.

These batteries were blazing away a few minutes before 10 a.m. when an aide from General McClellan galloped up to Burnside with the long-awaited orders to attack. The orders had been drafted at 9:10 a.m. — after the repulse of Hooker's I Corps and Mansfield's XII Corps, and while Sumner was leading one of Sedgwick's divisions to disaster in the West Woods. Before authorizing the orders, the cautious McClellan had waited until he had word that General Franklin's VI Corps was approaching the field from Pleasant Valley, thus providing reserves against the big Confederate counterattack McClellan expected at any moment. The orders promised support for Burnside once the bridge was captured.

Neither McClellan nor Burnside fully realized the extent to which Lee had stripped his southern flank. Burnside read the orders, apparently still under the impression that his role was diversionary, that he was to attempt something less than a full-scale advance. Then he passed the orders on to Cox, who hurried off to execute the plan he and Burnside had earlier agreed upon.

Their idea was to hit Toombs's defenders by assaulting the bridge and by fording the Antietam a half mile downstream. Brigadier General Isaac Rodman — a 40-year-old Rhode Island Quaker whose middle name was Peace — took his own division and a brigade from Cox's old Kanawha Division downstream to look for the ford McClellan's engineers had selected the previous day. The other Kanawha brigade of three Ohio regiments under Brigadier General George Crook was chosen to carry the bridge — a compliment from Burnside for their vigorous opening attack at South Mountain on Sunday. They were to be supported by Brigadier General Samuel Sturgis' division.

The stickiest job fell to the 11th Connecticut. Assigned as skirmishers for the assault on the bridge, these men had to gain a foothold on that narrow span so Crook's Ohioans could cross over.

The commander of the 11th was Colonel Henry W. Kingsbury, a highly regarded 1861 graduate of West Point. Kingsbury's father had been an Army officer and a close friend of General Burnside's; his sister was married to Confederate General Simon Bolivar Buckner.

The young colonel formed his regiment behind the crest of a hill about 200 yards from the bridge and gave the order to advance. As soon as his line emerged from the trees on the crest, the Confederates opened fire. The Connecticut right was quickly pinned down, but two companies on the left reached the road alongside the creek and inched toward the bridge.

On his own initiative, Captain John D. Griswold led his men down into the creek. The water was about four feet deep, and the current was swift and roiled by enemy bullets. Most of the men turned back. Griswold, hit at midstream, struggled on. He reached the far bank, then slumped over, mortally wounded.

Other members of the regiment charged for the bridge, with Kingsbury up front urging them on. But the Confederate fire was too heavy, and slowly the Connecticut men fell back. In less than 15 minutes, the 11th lost 139 men, a third of its strength. Among the casualties was Colonel Kingsbury, shot four times; the last wound, in his stomach, proved fatal.

The main assault by Crook's brigade went awry from the start. Crook had failed to

Three Federals chat on the Burnside Bridge in a post-battle photograph taken from the wooded bluff on Antietam Creek's west bank, which was occupied by Georgia troops during the fighting. When the Federals emerged from the tree line beyond the field on the far bank, the Confederates opened a murderous fire.

Colonel Henry W. Kingsbury of the 11th Connecticut was mortally wounded leading the first charge on the Burnside Bridge. So highly regarded was the 25-year-old officer that General Ambrose Burnside issued a proclamation mourning his death. A West Point classmate wrote that Kingsbury had embarked on "a career which nothing but death could terminate in failure."

examine the terrain that his brigade had occupied for nearly two days. Consequently, instead of storming over the ridge and down the hillside to the bridge, Crook blundered into a strip of woods. When his men finally reached the creek, they were a quarter of a mile upstream from the bridge. There, they lay on the east bank and exchanged volleys with the Confederate skirmishers across the Antietam.

Downstream, General Rodman's force was also having problems. The ford McClellan's engineers had selected the previous day had such steep banks that it turned out to be unusable. Rodman sent a couple of companies farther downstream in search of a crossing known as Snavely's Ford, which some local farmers had mentioned.

While waiting to hear news of Rodman's progress, Burnside and Cox prepared a second attack against the bridge. They selected a brigade of four regiments from Sturgis' division. This time there would be little danger of the men getting lost, for the lead two regiments — the 2nd Maryland and 6th New Hampshire — were lined up in column of fours and pointed down the road that ran alongside the creek to the bridge. Here, however, they presented easy targets for sharpshooters on the other side. Before the Federal column could even get near the bridge, the attack fell apart.

It was now noon, and McClellan was growing exasperated. From his headquarters two miles away, he sent a succession of couriers to light a fire under Burnside. McClellan ordered one aide, "Tell him if it costs 10,000 men he must go now."

Shortly after noon, McClellan's inspector general, Colonel Delos B. Sackett, arrived at Burnside's headquarters with orders from

Major General Ambrose E. Burnside, the affable but incompetent commander of the Federal IX Corps, had no pretensions to military genius. "He was not fitted to command," a fellow general once remarked. "No one knew this better than himself."

the commanding general "to push forward the troops without a moment's delay." Sackett was under instructions to remain with Burnside until these orders from McClellan were carried out. Burnside was indignant. "McClellan appears to think I am not trying my best to carry this bridge," he complained to Sackett. "You are the third or fourth one who has been to me this morning with similar orders."

For a third attempt to take the bridge, Burnside called on Sturgis' other brigade, commanded by Colonel Edward Ferrero. A dapper little former dancing master at West Point, Ferrero had finessed his way to high rank, making use of his connections at Tammany Hall, the powerful New York City political and social club. Aside from possessing what one of his soldiers called "a

Brigadier General Robert Toombs, the fiery former Georgia politician who led the defense of the Burnside Bridge, scorned his West Point-trained colleagues for being excessively cautious. He claimed that if the Confederacy ever fell, its epitaph should be: "Died of West Point."

stentorian voice, which, on brigade drill, could be heard almost from one end of the line to the other," Ferrero lacked most of the attributes of good military leadership. But he did have among his four regiments a pair of especially good ones, the 51st New York and the 51st Pennsylvania, both with able commanders.

Ferrero got his regiments in line and gave a speech. "It is General Burnside's special request that the two 51sts take that bridge," he boomed. "Will you do it?"

The question caught the men by surprise. Few of them had much respect for Ferrero. The Pennsylvanians were particularly offended because he had recently denied them the privilege of receiving their daily shot of whiskey.

A few moments passed, and then Corporal

Lewis Patterson of the 51st Pennsylvania piped up: "Will you give us our whiskey, Colonel, if we take it?"

"Yes, by God," thundered Ferrero, "you shall have as much as you want!"

The soldiers had this promise — and some strong artillery support. Two Federal batteries moved closer to the creek at a point upstream where they could enfilade the enemy defenders. And Crook's men wrestled down the hillside a light howitzer that they had captured from the Confederates in an earlier battle. This piece began pumping double charges of canister across the creek.

Ferrero's two attacking regiments formed side by side behind the crest of the hill near the bridge. The formation was intended to enable the two regiments to cross the bridge four men abreast, then turn left and right to form into lines of battle.

About 12:30 p.m. they mounted the crest and, bayonets fixed, started down the slope at the double-quick. Halfway down the hill, men began to fall. Enemy fire rose to such intensity that the neat Federal columns were quickly broken up; the troops raced to seek cover near the bridge.

Colonel Robert Potter's New Yorkers ran to the left, just downstream from the bridge, and suffered heavy losses trying to take shelter behind a rail fence that afforded scant protection. On the right, north of the bridge, some of the Pennsylvanians tore down a section of fence and piled up the rails for cover. Others ducked behind a stone wall that ran along the creek.

The Federals were now scarcely 25 yards from the enemy, and firing from behind fence and wall. "The way we showered the lead across that creek was nobody's business," recalled Lieutenant George W.

Whitman of the 51st New York, brother of poet Walt Whitman.

Behind the wall north of the bridge, Colonel John F. Hartranft, the 31-year-old commander of the Pennsylvanians, was urging his men on. His voice practically gone from yelling, he could only wave his hat and rasp, "Come on, boys, for I can't halloo any more."

A few minutes before 1 p.m., as the Confederate fire slackened, Captain William Allebaugh responded to his colonel's hoarse entreaties. He dashed onto the bridge. His first sergeant, two color-bearers and the color guard followed him. Then, in a sudden rush, men from both regiments jammed onto the narrow span. The colors of the 51st Pennsylvania were halfway across the bridge, the regimental historian wrote, when "the enemy deserted their works and scattered and scampered over the hills like a huge drove of scared sheep."

In reality, the Confederate withdrawal from the west bank was carried out with remarkable order. Even before the Federals got onto the bridge, Toombs knew the game was up. His men had only a few cartridges remaining, and reports from downstream indicated that the large Federal force under General Rodman had found Snavely's Ford. In a matter of minutes, Rodman's men could sweep down upon Toombs's right flank and rear.

Toombs waited until the Federals in his front started across the bridge. Then he instructed his Georgians to pull back to a previously designated position a half mile to the rear. Yet one of his officers refused to give ground. Lieutenant Colonel William R. Holmes of the 2nd Georgia ran down to the edge of the Antietam and, shouting defi-

antly, brandished his sword at the onrushing Federals. There he fell, his body riddled by bullets.

The Georgians' perseverance had cost the Federals more than 500 casualties while they themselves took losses of fewer than 160. More important, they had stalled the already-delayed Federal attack on the southern flank for three full hours.

None of this diminished the pride of those brave Pennsylvanians and New Yorkers who finally carried the bridge. Several days would pass, however, before the Pennsylvanians received their reward. Colonel Ferrero got his recognition first — promotion to brigadier general — and he had to be reminded of the promise he had made. The troops were lined up for the promotion ceremony when the persistent Corporal Patterson muttered in a loud undertone, "How about that whiskey?" Only after this reminder were the Pennsylvanians able to "wet down" their commander's new star with the long-awaited keg.

As soon as the two 51sts had secured the crest overlooking the bridge, the rest of the men in Sturgis' division filed across. They linked up on the left with Rodman's force coming north from Snavely's Ford and on the right with Crook's brigade, which had found a crossing 250 yards above the bridge.

It was now a little after 1 p.m. At last the way was open for a full-scale assault on Lee's thin line south of Sharpsburg. Indeed, such an advance appeared to be McClellan's last chance for victory. McClellan had abandoned hope of breaking the Confederate northern flank, and the Federal drive in the center, around Bloody Lane, was bogging down. The advance on the south now had to be much more than a mere diversion, and

This regimental color was carried into battle by the 51st New York, which lost 19 killed and 68 wounded at Antietam. Most of them fell during the crossing of the Burnside Bridge.

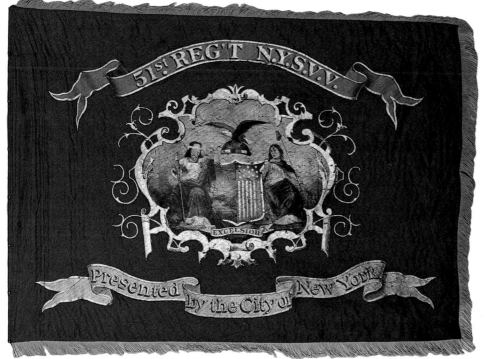

Colonels Robert Potter (*above*), of the 51st New York, and John Hartranft (*left*), of the 51st Pennsylvania, led the charge across the bridge. The two men had careers that ran oddly parallel. Both attended Union College at Schenectady, New York; their regiments fought together in the North Carolina expedition in early 1862; and both men eventually became generals.

McClellan sent yet another messenger to spur Burnside on.

But a new hitch developed. General Sturgis discovered that in his eagerness to carry the bridge he had neglected to arrange for a resupply of ammunition. He reported to Cox that his cartridge boxes were almost empty and, furthermore, his men were too worn out to continue the advance.

Cox accepted Sturgis' report and ordered his men replaced by the division of Brigadier General Orlando B. Willcox, which had been held in reserve all morning. But Willcox was three quarters of a mile behind the Antietam. It would take at least an hour for his three brigades to march across the hilly terrain to the creek. Then the troops would have to funnel across the bridge, a bottleneck that was already clogged with artillery caissons and ammunition wagons and under fire from enemy cannon. No one thought to use the ford discovered by Crook.

The lull that ensued on the southern flank coincided with the end of the fighting in the center. Lee had long since put in his last reserves, but he did take advantage of the early-afternoon respite to try to mount a counterstroke. The idea was to relieve the Federal pressure in the center and prevent an all-out attack in the south by creating a diversion on the northern flank. Far from the massive counterattack envisioned by McClellan, this would involve merely a column of cavalry led by Jeb Stuart and whatever guns and infantry Stonewall Jackson could spare from his depleted divisions. The force would try to swing wide to the northeast and outflank the Federal right.

To assess the odds, Jackson rode to the edge of the West Woods for a look at the Federal right flank. He asked for a volunteer to shinny up a tall hickory tree. Private William S. Hood of the 35th North Carolina stepped forward.

"How many troops are over there?" Jackson called up to young Hood.

"Oceans of them!" exclaimed Hood.

"Count the flags, sir!" Jackson said sternly.

Hood began counting the flags—two to each regiment, the Union and the regimental colors—while Federal sharpshooters popped away at his perch atop the tree. The flags Hood saw were those of Franklin's recently arrived VI Corps. When Hood reached the number 39, Jackson said: "That will do, come down, sir."

Undaunted by the prospect of facing at least 20 fresh Federal regiments, Jackson vowed to "drive McClellan into the Potomac." But as Stuart's column started off toward the north, it came up against a wall of Federal artillery arrayed on Joseph Poffen-

The Charge across the Burnside Bridge. Antietam. 1 P.M. Sept 17th 1862. Forbes

berger's farm. Reluctantly, Jackson called off the attack.

Lee, meanwhile, alerted to Burnside's build-up along the Antietam, ordered up every available cannon. The guns he collected included a dozen from Colonel Stephen Lee's battalion that had been refitted after withdrawing from the plateau in front of the Dunker Church that morning. Among them was a section from the unusual battery commanded by Captain William W. Parker. A physician by profession, Parker had recruited youngsters from his hometown of Richmond to man his guns. These boys ranged in age from 14 to 17, and after the morning's rigorous work, they were exhausted. Nonetheless, enough of them stepped forward to man a pair of guns on the heights just east of Sharpsburg.

In bolstering his right, Lee made no effort to strengthen General D. R. Jones's badly outnumbered division. To stop Burnside, Lee was counting on the arrival of a powerful column of reinforcements from Harpers Ferry: A. P. Hill's Light Division, so called for its mobility on the march and in battle.

Hill's division was the biggest in the Army of Northern Virginia, and arguably the best. Not the least of the reasons for its fine record was the fiery zest with which A. P. Hill led his men into the fray.

Lee's summons to hasten to Sharpsburg had reached Hill at Harpers Ferry at 6:30 that morning. Hill put on the red flannel shirt he always wore into battle and, an hour later, hurried out of town with five brigades, leaving one behind to gather up the captured booty. He took the route north along the west bank of the Potomac, the same one taken by Jackson.

Hill drove his men almost without a break in the heat and dust. His soldiers, after two days of harvesting the fruits of the big Federal commissary at Harpers Ferry, were better fed than anyone else in the Army of Northern Virginia. Many were also better dressed, having replaced their gray rags with brand-new blue uniforms.

At 2 p.m., the head of Hill's column reached Boteler's Ford and started across the Potomac. In six and a half hours, the troops had covered 15 miles. There were two miles yet to go.

Hill galloped his horse on ahead to Sharpsburg to report to Lee. Lee was so relieved to see him that he dropped his customary reserve and embraced his impetuous subordinate. It was 2:30 p.m., and Lee now had the reassurance that Hill's men were close at hand. But would they make it in time to stop Burnside?

Down at the bridge, Burnside was finally ready to advance. To make sure that he did, McClellan's high-ranking courier, Colonel Thomas Key, rode out from McClellan's headquarters with orders that would relieve Burnside of his command and replace him with Brigadier General George Morell of V Corps if Burnside failed to push ahead at once. McClellan could not bear to deliver such a rebuke to his old friend in person.

Burnside was not aware of the nature of Key's extraordinary mission. As it turned out, Key did not have to invoke McClellan's orders, for he could plainly see that Burnside was trying. The general had descended from his hilltop headquarters to direct traffic on the blood-slickened bridge that would be his monument.

By about 3 p.m. — two hours after the capture of the bridge — the entire IX Corps was across the Antietam and ready for the ad-

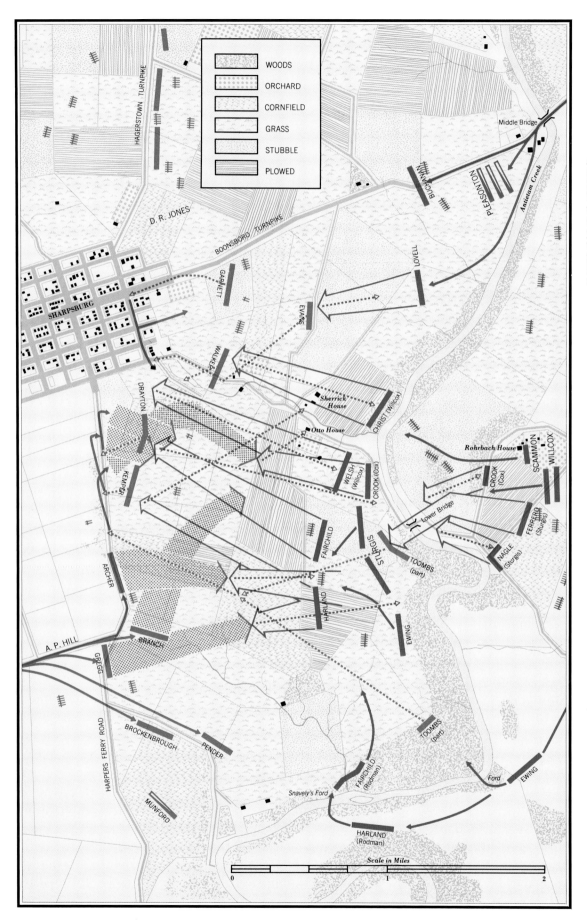

After the Federal brigades under Sturgis and Willcox crossed the Burnside Bridge, they were joined by Rodman's division, which had waded across Antietam Creek at Snavely's Ford. As the Federals pushed on toward Sharpsburg, they were attacked suddenly on the left flank by A. P. Hill's troops, who had just reached the battlefield after marching from Harpers Ferry.

WOODS

ORCHARD

CORNFIELD

GRASS

STUBBLE

PLOWED

HAGERSTOWN TURNPIKE

Middle Bridge

Antietam Creek

BUCHANAN

PLEASONTON

D. R. JONES

BOONSBORO TURNPIKE

LOVELL

GARNETT

EVANS

SHARPSBURG

WALKER

Sherrick House

CHRIST (Willcox)

DRAYTON

Otto House

SCAMMON

WILLCOX

Rohrbach House

KEMPER

WELSH (Willcox)

CROOK (Cox)

CROOK (Cox)

FERRERO (Sturgis)

FAIRCHILD

Lower Bridge

ARCHER

STURGIS

TOOMBS (part)

NAGLE (Sturgis)

HARLAND

A. P. HILL

BRANCH

GREGG

EWING

BROCKENBROUGH

PENDER

TOOMBS (part)

HARPERS FERRY ROAD

Ford

EWING

FAIRCHILD (Rodman)

Snavely's Ford

MUNFORD

HARLAND (Rodman)

Scale in Miles

0   1   2

vance. Willcox's division was on the Federal right with Crook's brigade in support; Rodman's division was on the left backed by the other Kanawha brigade. The plan was to converge on Sharpsburg, then block Lee's line of retreat west of the village.

Sturgis' men, who had carried the bridge, were held in reserve on the west bank. Even without Sturgis, however, the Federals had more than 8,000 troops, most of them fresh, and 22 cannon for close support. To a Confederate officer watching from the heights near Sharpsburg, the Federal advance, rolling forward on a front three quarters of a mile wide, was awe-inspiring. "The earth," he wrote "seemed to tremble beneath their tread."

On the Federal right, Willcox's two brigades started off astride the road that led from the bridge up toward Sharpsburg. The advance was spearheaded by the 79th New York, deployed in skirmish formation to the right of the road. These troops were the colorful Highlanders, a kilt-wearing militia unit before the War. In training camp in 1861, the Highlanders had staged a mutiny. McClellan had surrounded the rebellious regiment with tough Regulars and taken away the Highlanders' colors until they earned them back in combat. The colors were returned after the men acquitted themselves well in a skirmish near Falls Church, Virginia, in September 1861.

The terrain the Highlanders had to cover was fairly steep and relatively open farmland ascending in a series of crests and hollows to the high ground around Sharpsburg. The attackers soon discovered that almost every haystack and fence concealed enemy skirmishers and that the heights above, and to the right, bristled with Confederate cannon.

Major General Ambrose Powell Hill, commander of the Light Division, had a gentlemanly exterior that hid a fighting spirit. "At the critical moment," wrote an admiring comrade, "Hill was always at his strongest."

About halfway between the Burnside Bridge and Sharpsburg, the Highlanders encountered strong resistance from skirmishers firing from the cover of stone walls on the farm of Joseph Sherrick. (One of the walls also hid the 60-year-old farmer's life savings of $3,000 in gold, which he recovered after the battle.) The Federals flushed the skirmishers, but as they pushed on to higher ground about 200 yards beyond the Sherrick farmhouse, they ran into their first substantial body of enemy infantry. A brigade of South Carolinians came down the southern slope of Cemetery Hill, where Confederate artillery was concentrated, and met the advancing Federals in an apple orchard. A two-gun section of Massachusetts artillery helped blast the Confederates out, however, and Federal infantry followed with the bayonet. The South Carolinians pulled

131

back behind a stone wall at the southeastern edge of Sharpsburg.

By now, the Confederate guns on Cemetery Hill were in jeopardy. These batteries were threatened on their right by Willcox's advance and in front by several battalions of Regular Army infantry from Porter's V Corps that had crossed the middle bridge over the Antietam to support Federal batteries along the Boonsboro pike. The Confederate guns, along with the little brigade of Virginians supporting them, had to leave the hill and retreat back into town.

At this juncture, with his skirmishers less than 200 yards from Sharpsburg, Willcox called a halt. Ammunition was running low, and he wanted to wait for the supply wagons to catch up.

Meanwhile, in the rolling hills farther south, the left wing of IX Corps, Rodman's

division, had launched its westward advance toward the Harpers Ferry Road. The brigade under Colonel Harrison Fairchild led off. From the start, his three regiments faced a fury of shellfire from a dozen enemy guns mounted on a ridge a half mile or so ahead.

Fairchild's right wing, the men of the 9th New York, presented distinctive targets. They were Zouaves, wearing tasseled red fezzes and dark blue uniforms trimmed with magenta braid.

The founder of the 9th New York, Colonel Rush Hawkins, was home on leave, but the regiment was in capable hands. Lieutenant Colonel Edgar A. Kimball was a former newspaper editor, and a tough veteran of the Mexican War. He led the Zouaves forward through the bombardment, pausing periodically under the protection of a low ridge to dress his line, clap his hands and shout,

The 9th New York Zouaves drive back a Confederate regiment from a stone-and-rail fence on the high ground in front of Sharpsburg. The charge marked the Federal high-water mark during the battle; shortly afterward, a Confederate counterattack forced the Zouaves to withdraw.

"Bully Ninth! Bully Ninth! Boys, I'm proud of you! Every one of you!"

On they went, men falling at every step. A single shell wiped out eight Zouaves. Lieutenant Matthew Graham glanced back and saw the field "sprinkled all over with our dead and wounded." He noticed that the fallen all lay with their heads toward the enemy, reminding him of cornstalks that had been "rolled down to lie in the same direction for convenience in plowing them under."

When the Zouaves reached the last slope leading up the gun-infested ridge, two Confederate batteries limbered up and withdrew to keep from being overrun. But two small brigades of Confederate infantry remained behind a stone wall and a rail fence.

Major General David R. "Neighbor" Jones, whose division held the Confederate right flank, may well have been a casualty of the battle even though he was unhurt in the fighting. A victim of heart disease, Jones suffered a massive stroke soon after Antietam and died in January 1863.

One of the Confederates, waiting with his musket resting on the lower rail of a fence, was Private Alexander Hunter of the 17th Virginia. Earlier, Hunter had remarked to a comrade about the "peculiar tuneful pitch in the flight" of Minié balls. "A musical ear," he decided, "can study the different tones as they skim through the space."

Hunter now sighted his musket about two feet above the crest in front of him and listened as Fairchild's three big Federal regiments tramped up the hill. Hunter's regiment numbered a mere 55 men, and the other Confederate regiments there were nearly as thin.

"The first thing we saw appear," recalled Hunter, "was the gilt eagle that surmounted the pole, then the top of the flag, next the flutter of the Stars and Stripes; then their hats came in sight; still rising, the faces emerged; next a range of curious eyes appeared, then such a hurrah as only the Yankee troops could give broke the stillness, and they surged towards us."

Not until the Federal bayonets flashed above the crest 50 feet away did Private Hunter and his mates open fire. The Federal lines staggered, recovered, and returned volley after volley.

The colors of the 9th New York fell to the ground. Zouaves rushed to retrieve the banner, and in rapid succession seven would-be color-bearers fell dead or wounded. Finally Captain Adolph Libaire seized the flag and swung it around his head. "Up, damn you, and forward," he shouted to his company. The Zouaves responded with their war cry, "Zou! Zou! Zou!" and surged toward the Confederate line.

One of the Zouave officers made it to the stone wall on the right and mounted it. With

The Lutheran church on Main
Street in Sharpsburg shows damage
from Federal artillery fire. During the battle, the Confederates
used the church as a signal station;
by the time this photograph was
taken, in late September 1862, the
building housed a hospital.

his kepi perched on the point of his sword he waved his men forward. Flashing their bayonets and using their muskets as clubs, the Federals broke through the thin Confederate defense line.

The two Confederate brigades were badly mauled. The little 17th Virginia lost 31 killed or wounded and 10 captured, including Alexander Hunter. With Federals in pursuit, the survivors ran down the hill into Sharpsburg. "Oh, how I ran!" wrote Private John Dooley of the 1st Virginia. "I was afraid of being struck in the *back*, and I frequently turned around in running, so as to avoid if possible so disgraceful a wound."

Sharpsburg now seethed with a sense of impending disaster. Confederate stragglers choked the streets as ambulances clattered past, leaking blood through the floorboards. Civilians huddled in their cellars while Federal shells smashed brick and glass, and in the smoke-shrouded sky flocks of frightened pigeons flew in circles. A young girl from a pro-Union family later recalled the view from her attic window: "On all the distant hills around were the blue uniforms and shining bayonets of our men and I thought it was the prettiest sight I ever saw in my life."

A few impatient Federal skirmishers even prowled the streets on the outskirts of town. Willcox's division held the high ground to the southeast. On the hill a few hundred yards south of town, the Zouaves of Fairchild's brigade needed only to thrust three quarters of a mile farther west to sever the Confederate line of retreat to Boteler's Ford on the Potomac.

Lee's right was in shreds. Of the five brigades in D. R. Jones's division, only Toombs's unit was still intact. After pulling back from the bridge, Toombs's three regiments had been reinforced by two regiments brought up from the rear. His brigade was now backed up against the Harpers Ferry Road a half mile south of Sharpsburg, facing the Federal far left. With roughly 700 men, Toombs did not have a prayer of stemming the Federal tide. And Longstreet, commanding the Confederate center and right, could shift no reinforcements from the battered center.

The only hope was the Light Division of A. P. Hill. Where was it? From his headquarters just west of Sharpsburg, Lee kept looking to his right for some sign. The only troops he could see there were the long blue lines of Burnside's advancing Federals.

Then, about 3:30 p.m., Lee noticed a distant column of troops off to the southeast. One of his artillery officers, Lieutenant John A. Ramsay, happened to ride by carrying a telescope. Lee stopped him and asked Ramsay to identify the column.

Ramsay focused his telescope and said, "They are flying the United States flag."

Lee pointed to another line of men farther to the right. "What troops are those?"

Ramsay focused again and reported, "They are flying the Virginia and Confederate flags."

"It is A. P. Hill from Harpers Ferry," said Lee without a trace of emotion. Then he rode off to watch Hill's advance.

Hill had 3,000 men, hundreds more having fallen by the wayside from exhaustion on the furious march that had brought the division 17 miles in eight hours. From the Potomac, his column had made straight for Sharpsburg, cutting northeast across the countryside and then picking up a little farm lane that led to the Harpers Ferry Road. The column turned onto the road just south of Toombs's position.

Hill then divided his column. To guard his right flank, he sent two brigades off to the southeast. The other three brigades, about 2,000 men, filed in on the right of Toombs's regiments and prepared to attack.

Hill could not have chosen a better spot. Here, on their extreme left, the Federals were most vulnerable. The southernmost brigade in Rodman's division — led by Colonel Edward Harland — had failed to keep pace with the Zouaves and the other regiments to the north. Only one of Harland's regiments, the 8th Connecticut, had heard their brigade commander give the order

The indomitable Clara Barton cut through official red tape and the conventions of society to become an unofficial field nurse with the Army of the Potomac. She served so close to the front lines at Antietam that on one occasion a stray bullet passed through her sleeve, killing a soldier she was caring for.

to advance. While these men pushed west against Toombs's infantry, forcing the Confederates to abandon three guns, the rest of Harland's brigade — the 16th Connecticut and the 4th Rhode Island — lagged behind. The resulting gap was a perfect opening for Hill's attack.

Just a few minutes before Hill struck, Rodman saw the Confederates coming and sent an aide ahead to alert the green 16th Connecticut, which was just then moving west into farmer John Otto's cornfield. Then Rodman galloped forward to warn Colonel Fairchild's brigade. Crossing a meadow he was mortally wounded in the chest by a Confederate sharpshooter. Rodman was the ninth Union general to fall that day.

At 3:40 p.m., Hill's troops struck the Otto cornfield. Leading the attack was Brigadier General Maxcy Gregg's brigade of South Carolinians. Such was Gregg's sense of urgency that he did not take the time to shift his men from column of fours into a conventional line of battle but simply shouted, "Commence firing, men, and form the line as you fight."

The men of the 16th Connecticut had never been under fire before. In service only three weeks, they did not know the first thing about maneuvering on a battlefield. Until the previous evening, many of them had never even loaded their muskets. They were approaching a ravine that divided the 40-acre cornfield from north to south when they heard a suspicious rustling in the cornstalks. Then from front and left flank, recalled B. F. Blakeslee of the 16th, "volley after volley in quick succession was hurled into our midst."

The Connecticut men gamely returned the fire, but they were outmatched. Within a few minutes, 185 of them went down, and their line disintegrated. The 4th Rhode Island came up on the right, but by now the battle lines were so close — 30 to 40 yards apart — that the Rhode Islanders hardly knew where to fire. In the high corn it was hard to distinguish between friend and foe. The fact that some of the Confederates were wearing Federal uniforms picked up at Harpers Ferry only added to the confusion.

At one point the Rhode Islanders even mistook the blue flag of the 1st South Carolina for the Stars and Stripes. They stopped firing while two officers and the regiment's color-bearer went forward for a closer look. The little delegation was 20 feet from the Confederate line when the South Carolinians unleashed a volley, killing the color-bearer. Soon, reported Colonel Daniel H. Hamilton of the 1st South Carolina, his men were firing so rapidly that the rounds fouled their rifles,

and they were "obliged to use stones to hammer the charges down."

First the Connecticut troops broke and ran, then the Rhode Islanders. The rout in the cornfield left Harland's lead regiment, the 8th Connecticut, far out in advance and isolated. Upon its front and flank fell another of A. P. Hill's brigades and some of Toombs's men. The Confederates recovered the captured guns and drove the Connecticut men down the hills toward Antietam Creek.

General Cox, trying to mend this major break in his left, sent up regiments from the Kanawha Division. At a stone wall near Otto's cornfield, the Ohioans collided with all three of Hill's attacking brigades and, outflanked, quickly fell back.

There was a pause in the action, and Hill summoned his brigade commanders to a conference. The four generals and their staffs soon attracted the fire of enemy sharpshooters. As Hill's senior brigadier, General Lawrence O'Bryan Branch of North Carolina, was lifting his binoculars to his eyes, a bullet passed through his head. Branch was killed, the ninth Confederate general to fall.

Hill's attack had broken the Federal far left. Cox, fearing that Hill might now turn on the exposed flank of his forward brigades, ordered their withdrawal. About 5 p.m. the orders reached Willcox, who was waiting for ammunition on the outskirts of Sharpsburg. One of Willcox's aides then passed the word to the 9th New York Zouaves on the left.

These Zouaves were now all alone on the hill overlooking Sharpsburg. The other two regiments in Fairchild's brigade already had wheeled to the left and pulled back 250 yards to hold the flank against Hill. The Zouaves had lost more than a third of their men killed or wounded. Nonetheless, Lieutenant Colonel Kimball appealed for re-inforcements. He still had more than 100 able-bodied men, and he wanted to advance, not retreat. When one of his own officers called his attention to the shortage of cartridges, Kimball replied: "We have the bay-onets. What are they for?"

Only after Willcox came to Kimball and personally ordered him to withdraw did the colonel yield. As the Zouaves formed to march to the rear, giving up the high ground they had fought so gallantly to gain, Kimball told Willcox: "Look at my regiment! They go off this field under orders. They are not driven off. Do they look like a beaten regiment?"

Burnside's IX Corps had suffered casualties of about 20 per cent, but he still fielded more than 8,500 men — twice the number of enemy troops confronting him. Yet Burn-

Dr. Anson Hurd (*left*), regimental surgeon for the 14th Indiana Volunteers, attends Confederate wounded lying in improvised tents at a Federal field hospital set up on Otho Smith's farm, two miles northeast of Sharpsburg. The barn, farmhouse and outbuildings shown in the panoramic view below housed Federal wounded from French's division.

side and Cox pulled the corps all the way back to the west bank of the Antietam, to the heights overlooking the bridge.

Then, beset by doubts that he could hold even the bridge, Burnside dispatched a message to McClellan asking for more men and guns. McClellan, who had reneged on his morning vow to support his old friend's advance, promised him just one battery. "I can do nothing more," said McClellan. "I have no infantry."

In fact, McClellan nearly had the battle won — but he did not realize it. He still had Porter's V Corps in reserve, along with Franklin's VI Corps, and if he had but dared to fling them against Lee's exhausted, thin line, victory would have been his. But he was so stunned by his staggering losses and worried about the possibility of a massive counterattack that he refused to commit them. In the center, along the Boonsboro pike, only a single Confederate brigade — that of Nathan Evans — stood between Porter and a breakthrough into Sharpsburg. Longstreet wrote later: "We were so badly crushed that at the close of the day ten thousand fresh troops could have come in and taken Lee's army and everything in it." McClellan had twice that many troops who had scarcely fired a shot all day.

The extraordinary depth of McClellan's caution — and that of his chief subordinates — had been revealed earlier that afternoon, about the time of A. P. Hill's devastating attack. One of Porter's Regulars, Captain Hiram Dryer, was leading his battalion of the 4th U.S. Infantry west of the middle bridge on the Boonsboro Turnpike. Dryer got near enough to the village to see how vulnerable the enemy defenses were in

Several days after the battle, Federal soldiers relax behind a dead tree on Samuel Mumma's farm. At the foot of the tree is the grave of Private John Marshall of the 28th Pennsylvania, who was killed during the Confederate counterattack out of the West Woods.

front of Sharpsburg. He suggested a head-on attack in the center, and his proposal was relayed up the chain of command to his division commander, Brigadier General George Sykes.

When the proposal reached George Sykes, he conferred with McClellan and Porter. Sykes said later that McClellan seemed inclined to approve the attack. But Porter, according to Sykes, shook his head and said to McClellan, "Remember, General, I command the last reserve of the last Army of the Republic."

There it rested. Burnside held on to his bridge. A. P. Hill, outnumbered, was in no position to press the issue. He had saved the day for Lee's army, and in doing so, had saved perhaps the Confederacy itself.

By 5:30 p.m., the hard fighting had ended on the heights overlooking the Burnside Bridge. After 12 hours, the Battle of Antietam was over, although random firing continued for another hour or so while men prayed for darkness to put a stop to the slaughter.

Night did come and with it a mournful chorus of agony rising from the lantern-lit barns and houses where surgeons sawed at mangled limbs, and from the pitch-black hollows, woods and fields where wounded men lay beyond reach of help.

Near midnight, Stonewall Jackson's young aide Henry Kyd Douglas rode on an errand up to the West Woods not far from where the battle had begun at dawn. He found himself in a field, one of many where the fighting had swept back and forth.

"The dead and dying lay as thick over it as harvest sheaves," Douglas recalled. "The pitiable cries for water and appeals for help were much more horrible to listen to than the deadliest sounds of battle. Silent were the dead, and motionless. But here and there were raised stiffened arms; heads made a last effort to lift themselves from the ground; prayers were mingled with oaths, the oaths of delirium; men were wriggling over the earth; and midnight hid all distinction between the blue and the grey.

"My horse trembled under me in terror, looking down at the ground, sniffing the scent of blood, stepping falteringly as a horse will over or by the side of human flesh; afraid to stand still, hesitating to go on, his animal instinct shuddering at this cruel human mystery. Once his foot slid into a little shallow filled with blood and spurted a little stream on his legs and my boots. I had had a surfeit of blood that day and I couldn't stand this. I dismounted and giving the reins to my courier I started on foot into the wood of Dunker Church."

A GALLERY OF THE DEAD

In October 1862, Mathew Brady put on display at his New York City gallery a series of photographs that ended once and for all the general public's romantic notions of the War. Taken at Antietam by Brady's colleague Alexander Gardner, the pictures were the first ever of dead Americans on a field of battle; that the corpses were all nameless Confederates made no difference in the impact of Gardner's images. "Let him who wishes to know what war is look at this series of illustrations," Dr. Oliver Wendell Holmes Sr. wrote. Another viewer said: "We recognized the battlefield as a reality, but a remote one, like a funeral next door. Mr. Brady has brought home the terrible earnestness of war. If he has not brought bodies and laid them in our dooryards, he has done something very like it."

CONFEDERATE SLAIN ON THE FIELD

BODIES GATHERED FOR BURIAL NEAR THE WEST WOODS

THOSE KILLED BESIDE A FENCE ALONG THE HAGERSTOWN PIKE

CONFEDERATE DEAD NEAR BURNSIDE BRIDGE

"And Here We Lie"

On the morning of September 18, the men of the opposing armies stared warily at one another across the littered field. Here and there a few pickets traded shots, but neither side made a serious attempt to resume the fighting. Federal and Confederate units worked out informal truces and began to gather up the wounded and the dead. The corpses already were beginning to blacken and bloat in the hot September sun. "Many were as black as Negroes," declared a shaken Federal officer, "heads and faces hideously swelled, covered with dust until they looked like clods. Their attitudes were wild and frightful."

Lieutenant George F. Noyes, one of Brigadier General Abner Doubleday's staff officers, was astounded by the carnage he witnessed: "No matter in what direction we turned, it was all the same shocking picture, awakening awe rather than pity, benumbing the senses rather than touching the heart, glazing the eye with horror rather than filling it with tears."

Smashed caissons, broken wheels, dismounted cannon, muskets, blankets, haversacks, canteens were everywhere, strewn by what one soldier called "the awful tornado of battle." Around the surgeons' tables in the barn of the Roulette farm, amputated arms and legs were piled several feet deep. Vultures and crows circled overhead, waiting for an opportunity to descend to earth. "Most troublesome," declared Federal Brigadier General Oliver O. Howard, "was the atmosphere that arose from the swollen bodies of the dead horses. We tried piling rails and loose limbs of trees upon them and setting the heap on fire. This made the stench only increase in volume."

Never before had so many Americans fallen in combat in a single day. By the best available counts, casualties numbered 22,726. Federal losses accounted for somewhat more than half: 2,108 killed, 9,549 wounded and 753 missing, for a total of 12,410. The Confederates lost 1,546 killed, 7,752 wounded and 1,018 missing, for a total of 10,316. Appalling as these statistics were, they underestimated the actual cost, for vast numbers of the wounded would later die of their injuries, and many of the missing were dead.

One in every four men engaged in the battle had fallen — and for what? A great deal, as events would soon make clear; for the Battle of Antietam, or Sharpsburg as the Confederates referred to it, proved to be a turning point in the War, profoundly altering the terms under which the conflict would be fought.

But the fateful consequences were not evident in the immediate aftermath. Tactically, the battle was a standoff. The Federals had gained ground, but they had failed to dislodge Lee's army from the ridge in front of Sharpsburg. The sheer uselessness of the effort was a bitter bounty for the soldiers of both sides. The words of one wounded Confederate captured that sense of futility.

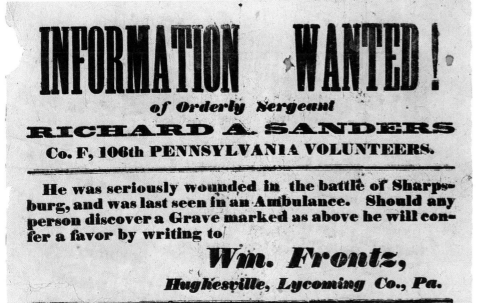

INFORMATION WANTED!

of Orderly Sergeant

RICHARD A. SANDERS

Co. F, 106th PENNSYLVANIA VOLUNTEERS.

He was seriously wounded in the battle of Sharpsburg, and was last seen in an Ambulance. Should any person discover a Grave marked as above he will confer a favor by writing to

Wm. Frontz,

Hughesville, Lycoming Co., Pa.

Printed by F. H. Irwin, Odd Fellow Office, Boonsboro', where all kinds of Printing is done.

A handbill posted in Sharpsburg after the battle seeks information about a missing Pennsylvania soldier. The Federal government had no formal system for notifying next of kin that a man had been killed or wounded; the bad news often came through a newspaper casualty list or a letter from a comrade of the victim.

Colonel Norman J. Hall of the 7th Michigan told of pausing in the Cornfield on the day of the battle to console an injured Mississippian. "You fought and stood well," Hall said to him. "Yes," responded the Southerner, "and here we lie."

Lee briefly entertained the notion on the 18th of trying again to turn the Federal right. But he soon gave it up. His staggering losses made any further operations risky at best. And, he needed time to evacuate his wounded, feed and rest his men, collect stragglers and remove the captured guns and supplies down at Harpers Ferry.

McClellan refused to attack because he was McClellan. Despite the arrival of Major General Darius Couch's division from Pleasant Valley and Brigadier General Andrew Humphreys' division from Frederick — 14,000 fresh men, which again brought his numerical advantage to almost 2 to 1 — McClellan decided that "the success of an attack was not certain." Once again, his fear of losing prevented him from reaching for near-certain victory. "One battle lost, and almost all would have been lost," he wrote. "Lee's army might then have marched as it pleased on Washington, Baltimore, Philadelphia, or New York."

Lee did march that night, but to the rear. Nothing could be gained by remaining in Maryland, the general realized, and his scouts had reported the arrival of the fresh Federal divisions.

The Confederates moved out on the road to Shepherdstown. They had to leave their dead and most severely wounded for the Federals to cope with; it was anguishing, but there was no alternative. The supply wagons were the first to roll, followed by ambulances carrying those wounded who could be transported. Then came the infantry, plodding the three miles southwestward to the Potomac in a fine rain that turned the dust into mire.

At Boteler's Ford, a mile or so downriver from Shepherdstown, cavalry sentinels stood with flaming torches to light the crossing into Virginia. It was a melancholy scene, in sharp contrast to those sunny days two weeks before when Lee's invading army had splashed across the river nearly 50 miles downstream. Then the regimental bands had played round after round of "Maryland, My Maryland." Now, when the band of the 18th Mississippi struck up that familiar tune, the soldiers shouted it down. They wanted to hear "Carry Me Back to Old Virginny."

Lee anxiously remained near the ford through most of the night. The narrow country lane leading down to the river was clogged with wagons and horses, and he knew what havoc the Federal artillery could

wreak upon this bottleneck if McClellan chose to give pursuit.

Near dawn on Friday, September 19, astride his horse in the waist-deep water, Lee saw General John Walker ride down to the river. Walker's division was bringing up the rear, and Lee asked what part of the army remained behind. When Walker replied that everything had crossed except a battery of artillery and some wagons bearing the wounded, Lee gave vent to the strain he had been under throughout the night. "Thank God!" he exclaimed.

Lee need not have worried. Though the Federal pickets in front of Sharpsburg had heard the unmistakable sounds of retreat — the cadence of marching feet, the rumble of caissons — McClellan had made no attempt to disrupt the withdrawal.

That morning McClellan found the field in front of him empty of all but the dead and dying. He sent forward his cavalry, followed by Porter's V Corps, to seek out Lee. The cavalry reached Boteler's Ford about 8 a.m., just in time to glimpse the grayclad columns vanishing in the distance on the Virginia side of the river.

But the Confederate rear guard was closer at hand. Deployed on the steep bluffs overlooking the Potomac from the south bank,

Under white flags, a Federal and a Confederate officer shake hands near the Dunker Church during an impromptu truce called to allow both sides to collect their dead and wounded. Many such arrangements were made on the day after the battle.

and in the rolling fields beyond, were 44 pieces of artillery supported by two brigades of infantry. Lee had left them there to guard the ford at least until sundown while his army moved toward Martinsburg, eight miles to the west.

The Federal cavalrymen brought up 18 guns from their horse artillery, and for two hours the opposing batteries engaged in a spirited duel. Then Porter approached with his V Corps and about noon deployed the 1st U.S. Sharpshooters in the dry bed of the Chesapeake & Ohio Canal, which paralleled the north bank of the river. From the cover of this convenient trench, the Federal marksmen started picking off the Confederate cannoneers on the far bluff.

The Confederate rear guard was commanded by Lee's chief of artillery, Brigadier General William Nelson Pendleton, a 53-year-old West Point graduate who before the War had given up soldiering for the Episcopal priesthood. With his pale gray beard and hair, he resembled Lee. There the similarity ended.

Pendleton had never commanded infantry before, and he soon lost control. Not having bothered to count his troops (the two brigades had been thinned to a total of 600 men), he kept ordering forward numbers that did not exist. Toward dusk, as the Confederates began to fall back, taking their guns with them, a Federal raiding party of 500 volunteers crossed the ford and captured four of the cannon.

Pendleton, alone in the dark at his command post, feared that his losses were much worse. Panic-stricken, he rode back a few miles to the rear and, sometime after midnight, found Lee asleep under an apple tree. He woke the commanding general and blurt-

ed out a fearsome but absurd story of how the Federals had stormed the heights and seized all of his 44 guns.

"All?" exclaimed Lee.

"Yes, General, I fear all."

A staff officer lying nearby said the news "lifted me right off my blanket." But Lee received it with his customary composure. Nothing could be done until daylight, and he advised his rattled chief of artillery to get some sleep.

But Stonewall Jackson, disgusted with Pendleton, decided to take matters into his own hands. Jackson alerted A. P. Hill to be ready to march to the river at dawn with his division.

Jackson's move was timely. Though the Federal raiding party that had captured Pendleton's four guns had withdrawn to the Maryland shore during the night, McClellan decided to dispatch a much larger reconnaissance force, consisting of three brigades.

The lead Federal brigade, crack Regulars from Brigadier General George Sykes's division, crossed Boteler's Ford at 7 a.m. and headed southwest along the Charlestown Road. A mile or so beyond the river, Sykes's skirmishers collided with A. P. Hill's advancing Confederates. Outnumbered, Sykes pulled the brigade back to the bluffs by the river and then, on orders from Porter, withdrew across the Potomac with his brigade and another that had just been sent over.

Earlier, the third brigade in the Federal reconnaissance — under Colonel James Barnes — had crossed the ford into Virginia. Unaware of Sykes's situation, Barnes turned right along the river, passed an abandoned cement mill and dam a few hundred yards west of the ford and sent his most inexperienced regiment, the 118th Pennsylvania, up a ravine to the top of a sheer 80-foot-high cliff. The 118th Pennsylvania was known as the Corn Exchange Regiment because each of its recruits had received a $200 enlistment bonus from that Philadelphia exchange.

The Philadelphians, who had seen no action at Antietam, were forming their line of battle across the top of the cliff when less than a mile to their south appeared A. P. Hill's division, 5,000 men strong. The Confederates were advancing on a front three brigades wide, easily outflanking the 118th Pennsylvania on both sides.

There was still time for the 118th to pull out. In fact, Colonel Barnes was at that moment ordering the other regiments in the brigade to retreat. From the river road, one of Barnes's lieutenants frantically shouted up the ravine to Colonel Charles E. Prevost, commander of the 118th, urging him to withdraw his regiment. But Prevost stood on ceremony. "I do not receive orders in that way," he announced. "If Colonel Barnes has any order to give me, let his aide come to me."

The Confederates bore down on Prevost's untried troops, alone on the cliff. A well-placed barrage from Federal guns on the Maryland shore slowed Hill's veterans, but they continued to advance across the open ground, firing on the Philadelphians.

The men of the 118th gamely returned fire — or tried to. Their weapons were British Enfields, ordinarily dependable. Yet half of the men discovered to their horror that their rifles would not shoot. On many of these Enfields the mainspring was too weak to explode the percussion cap. In their excitement, several men failed to notice this defect, and they kept ramming new

cartridges down the barrel on top of the unexploded ones.

Castaway rifles and dead and wounded Federals quickly littered the ground. Some of the men snatched up weapons from their fallen comrades until they found one that would work. Others picked up stones and pounded frantically on the rifle hammer until the bullet fired.

Enemy troops were now only 50 yards away. One Confederate regiment worked its way over to the Federal right flank. When

Federal batteries on the Maryland shore of the Potomac fire over men of the 118th Pennsylvania to cover their withdrawal across the river near Boteler's Ford. The column at far right is retreating over the old mill dam.

Colonel Barnes to withdraw, all thoughts of gallantry gave way. "The scene that followed almost beggars description," admitted the regimental historians. "The brave men who had contended so manfully against these frightful odds broke in wild confusion for the river."

Some Federals were killed or maimed in the tumbling descent from the cliff. Most of the regiment funneled into the ravine, while the Confederates poured down fire from the heights. A fallen tree blocked the Federals' path. Attempting to climb over it, several Philadelphians became hopelessly entangled and were shot, their bodies dangling over the branches.

When the survivors reached the foot of the cliff near the river, they found the escape route to the ford downstream cut off by Confederate marksmen who were firing from the old cement mill. A small group of Federals sought shelter in the archways of some old lime-burning kilns dug into the base of the cliff, but there they soon came under fire from a friendly battery across the river whose crews had set their shell fuses too short.

Some men jumped into the river and began swimming. The Confederates took aim on them, and lifeless bodies were soon bobbing in the current. Lieutenant J. Rudhall White survived the 200-yard swim to the Maryland shore, crying as he climbed out of the water, "Thank God! I am over at last." At that moment a bullet plowed through his stomach, fatally wounding him.

Other Federals tried to scramble across the old mill dam, a partially submerged rock structure covered with rotting wood planks. William Madison took five bullets as he negotiated the slippery length of the dam. When the fifth bullet passed through his jaw,

the Philadelphians there changed front to meet this threat, their comrades in the center mistook the maneuver for a withdrawal and started to break. Colonel Prevost managed to restore his line by grabbing the regimental flag and waving it wildly. He was still flourishing it minutes later when a bullet smashed into his shoulder, putting him out of action.

Lieutenant Colonel James Gwyn assumed command, and for 30 minutes or more the Philadelphians held. But when an aide finally reached Gwyn with the order from he let out a howl of pain, then turned and fired a final shot. Terribly wounded, Madison nevertheless pulled through.

By 2 p.m., most of the Federal survivors had reached the Maryland shore, and Porter's sharpshooters, firing from the dry canal bed, forced the Confederates to withdraw.

Hill, exuberant at having literally driven the enemy off a cliff into the Potomac, bragged that it was "the most terrible slaughter that this war has yet witnessed. The broad surface of the Potomac was blue with the floating bodies of our foe." The lopsided battle had cost the 118th Pennsylvania Regiment 269 of its 750 men.

With his rear guard safe, Lee pulled back from the Potomac that night. Heartened by the outcome, he considered collecting his stragglers and renewing the invasion by crossing back into Maryland upstream at Williamsport. But Lee quickly realized, as he wrote President Davis a few days later, that his weary army had lost "its former temper and condition." Concluding that if he tried to invade Maryland again, "the hazard would be great and a reverse disastrous," Lee slowly withdrew to Winchester, in the Shenandoah Valley about 30 miles southwest of Sharpsburg.

McClellan let him go. He did send a large force across the Potomac to reoccupy Harpers Ferry, but the bulk of the army remained in Maryland. Any bold thoughts of pursuit had dissolved with the setback at Boteler's Ford. It reminded McClellan of a similar disaster at Ball's Bluff 11 months earlier. There as well, his men had been driven off a cliff and into the Potomac. Now, as then, the dramatic Confederate counterattack served to reinforce McClellan's innate caution. Before pursuing Lee south, he

must have time to reorganize and resupply.

Apart from the Boteler's Ford fiasco, known thereafter as the Battle of Shepherdstown, McClellan took pride in his recent accomplishments. To his wife he wrote, "Those in whose judgment I rely tell me that I fought the battle splendidly and that it was a masterpiece of art." McClellan's incredible good fortune in coming upon Lee's lost orders for the Maryland Campaign had helped, of course. And even then he had missed chance after chance to destroy the Confederate army.

Nonetheless, in a period of less than three weeks after taking control, the Federal commander had pulled together and transformed a defeated and dispirited army into an instrument powerful enough to repulse Lee's invasion of the North — the first time that the Army of Northern Virginia had ever been compelled to retreat. At South Mountain and Antietam, McClellan's Army of the Potomac had captured no fewer than 39 Confederate battle flags, more than had been claimed by Federal forces in any previous campaign. "Our victory was complete," McClellan wired General in Chief Henry Halleck. "The enemy is driven back into Virginia. Maryland and Pennsylvania are now safe."

With Lee's retreat, the true import of Antietam began to emerge. The Confederate withdrawal transformed a tactical stalemate into a strategic victory for the North. This victory was now seized upon by President Lincoln as the occasion to issue a document that would lend a new and deeper meaning to the bloodiest day in American history.

Back in July, Lincoln had prepared a first draft of the Emancipation Proclamation, decreeing freedom for the Confederacy's three

Federal officers who fought at Antietam relax on the grass at a campsite west of Sharpsburg. The group includes cavalry Brigadier General John Buford (*third from left*), Chief Surgeon John Letterman (*fifth from left*) and Brigadier General John Gibbon (*far right*), commander of the Iron Brigade. Seated behind the officers is the camp cook.

and a half million slaves. But the Federal armies were in retreat, and the timing awkward. Secretary of State William H. Seward urged Lincoln to put the proclamation aside, lest it be interpreted by the world as a sign of desperation — as Seward put it, "our last shriek on the retreat." The President agreed to wait for an improvement in military fortunes.

On Monday, September 22, five days after Antietam, Lincoln summoned the members of his Cabinet to the White House. He reminded them of the proclamation draft he had read to them in July. Before the Battle of Antietam, he went on, he had made a promise "to myself, and to my Maker" to

issue the proclamation if the Confederates were driven out of Maryland. "I think the time has come now. I wish that we were in a better condition. But the rebel army is now driven out, and I am going to fulfill that promise."

Though he personally opposed slavery, Lincoln's motives for the proclamation were more pragmatic than humanitarian. He wanted to sap a source of the Confederacy's economic strength by providing an incentive for slaves to escape. He wanted to repair the political schisms in the Republican Party, where a majority of Congressmen and Senators were in favor of abolition. And he wanted to forestall foreign intervention by

Soldiers of the 93rd New York, McClellan's headquarters guard, assemble in front of their tents near Sharpsburg after the battle. Eight months of hard campaigning had depleted their ranks from 998 officers and men to approximately 250.

appealing to world opinion. Thus Lincoln saw emancipation as a means of achieving his overriding goal of winning the War and preserving the Union. "I felt that we must change our tactics," he explained later, "or lose the game."

Lincoln issued the Emancipation Proclamation on grounds of "military necessity" under his powers as Commander in Chief. It pertained only to the slaves in the enemy homeland. The status of the slaves in the loyal border states of Kentucky, Maryland, Delaware and Missouri remained unchanged.

The proclamation was made public two days after the Cabinet meeting. It sparked outrage in the South, anger among conservative Democrats in the North and rejoicing among abolitionists like Ralph Waldo Emerson, who wrote: "It makes a victory of our defeats. Our hurts are healed; the health of the nation is repaired."

But such predictable responses would have less of an effect on the course of the War than would reactions from abroad. News of Antietam and Lee's failure to sustain his invasion was sufficient to discourage the British government from extending formal recognition to the Confederacy. Prime Minister Henry Palmerston wrote his Foreign Minister: "We must continue merely to be lookers-on till the war shall have taken a more decided turn." But, in the long run, it was the moral impact of emancipation that proved decisive in England and France. Abhorring slavery, the majority of the people in both countries shifted the weight of their opinion to the side of the Union, ensuring that their governments would remain neutral. Because of Antietam and the resulting Emancipation Proclamation, the

Confederacy would have to continue fighting alone, with no foreign help and little hope of it.

Lincoln shrewdly anticipated this favorable reaction abroad. He felt less certain about how emancipation would be perceived in the army that had made it possible. From McClellan on down, many officers in the Army of the Potomac were conservative Democrats who generally opposed immediate emancipation and favored a negotiated settlement with the Confederacy. This fact, as much as McClellan's penchant for caution, had created an extraordinary distrust of the generals among the Radical Republicans, who from the beginning of the War had

called for the abolition of slavery and an all-out war to destroy the South's institutions. These Radicals had repeatedly accused McClellan and some of his top officers of outright treason. After Antietam, they went so far as to circulate tales that McClellan had conspired with Lee to prevent a decisive Federal victory.

In addition to these rumors, a lot of loose talk was rattling around the Army of the Potomac itself. A few days after issuing the proclamation, Lincoln was confronted with the case of Major John Key, a member of Halleck's staff and, more importantly, brother of Colonel Thomas Key, McClellan's influential aide. After Antietam, John

GRAND SWEEPSTAKES FOR 1862.
Won by the Celebrated Horse "EMANCIPATION"

Emancipation. Old Abe 1.1.1. 'raband. C.S. 2.3.2. John Brown, J. A. 3.2.3. Philosopher. H.G. 4.4.4

Whipping the horse "Emancipation," President Lincoln is depicted in this Northern cartoon as having surged ahead of even the staunchest abolitionists on the question of freedom for slaves. Lincoln has out-distanced Massachusetts Senator Charles Sumner (*far left*), publisher William Lloyd Garrison (*second from left*), Massachusetts Governor John Andrew (*second from right*) and New York clergyman Henry Ward Beecher (*far right*).

Key had told another officer that McClellan failed to destroy Lee's army because "that is not the game. The object is that neither army shall get much advantage of the other; that both shall be kept in the field till they are exhausted, when we will make a compromise and save slavery."

Lincoln acted promptly and firmly. He fired Key as "an example and a warning" to officers who had loose tongues.

McClellan himself needed no such warning. To be sure, he thought the Emancipation Proclamation premature and believed that Lincoln had exceeded his presidential powers. "At one stroke of the pen," he protested in a letter to a friend, it changed "our free institutions into a despotism." He even briefly considered resigning his command because of it.

But McClellan was loyal. Even after prominent Democrats and a few fellow officers urged him to take a public stance against emancipation, he heeded calmer counsel and maintained a proper silence. And to quell disloyal talk among his men, he issued a general order — with a copy to the President — reminding them of the soldier's "highest duty" under the Constitution: "earnest support of the authority of the government."

What Lincoln wanted most of all from McClellan, however, was rapid and vigorous pursuit of the Confederates in Virginia. To help bring it about, he decided to pay a surprise visit to the general and his army.

The President arrived at Sharpsburg on October 1, looking, as one observer said, "careworn and troubled." Wearing a black suit and stovepipe hat, Lincoln visited field hospitals and reviewed the troops. He toured the Antietam battlefield in an ambulance,

sitting, a Federal officer noted, "with his long legs doubled up so that his knees almost struck his chin."

Lincoln devoted much of his three-day visit to prodding McClellan. He spoke to him of "overcautiousness" and pressed him to move the army forward. Yet McClellan afterward insisted that the President "was entirely satisfied with me and with all that I had done; that he would stand by me against all comers; that he wished me not to stir an inch until fully ready."

A story told by the President's close friend Ozias M. Hatch suggests that Lincoln must have sensed that he and McClellan were talking at cross-purposes. Early one morning during Lincoln's visit to Antietam, the President invited Hatch to go for a walk. On a hillside, Lincoln gestured in despair at the expanse of white tents spread out below them and inquired, "Hatch, Hatch, what is all of this?"

"Why, Mr. Lincoln," answered Hatch, "this is the Army of the Potomac."

"No, Hatch, no," replied Lincoln. "This is McClellan's bodyguard."

Having failed to persuade McClellan in their personal chats, Lincoln resorted to peremptory orders. On October 6, two days after Lincoln's return from Sharpsburg, General in Chief Halleck wired McClellan: "The President directs that you cross the Potomac and give battle to the enemy or drive him south. Your army must move now while the roads are good."

McClellan did not budge. He remained behind the Potomac, insisting in an increasingly bitter telegraphic duel with Washington that his army could not move without reinforcements and supplies. This long-range debate became so acrimonious that

President Lincoln meets with General McClellan (*sixth from left*) **and his staff at V Corps headquarters near Sharpsburg early in October 1862. Second from Lincoln's**

left is V Corps commander General Fitz-John Porter. At far right, wearing a slouch hat, is one of McClellan's aides-de-camp, Captain George Armstrong Custer.

when McClellan asked for more horses because those in his cavalry were broken down and plagued by a variety of diseases, Lincoln exploded. "I have just read your dispatch about sore-tongued and fatigued horses," the President wired caustically in reply. "Will you pardon me for asking what the horses of your army have done since the battle of Antietam that fatigues anything?"

McClellan's demands stemmed in part from his chronic perfectionism, from what one officer called his "incapacity of doing anything till an ideal completeness of preparation was reached." Nevertheless, some of McClellan's claims were valid. Colonel Charles S. Wainwright noted that more than half of the horses of the V Corps artillery were unshod and that a large number in all the batteries were lame with hoof rot. Many soldiers had been issued no new clothing since embarking on the Peninsular Campaign seven months before. Private Alfred Davenport of the 5th New York wrote of seeing "men with no coats, no underclothes, in rags, no shoes." When Lincoln reviewed Davenport's regiment at Antietam, the private added, "those who had overcoats were ordered to put them on, to hide the rags."

What McClellan failed to grasp, however, was that the Confederate Army was in even worse shape. And every day he delayed in pushing south enabled Lee's men to gain strength and numbers at their bivouacs near Winchester. By October 10, so many stragglers and recruits had joined the Army of Northern Virginia that Lee reported 64,273 present for duty. This was less than two thirds of McClellan's total but nearly double the number that had retreated from Sharpsburg three weeks before.

On October 9, Lee had launched Jeb Stuart and 1,800 cavalrymen on a daring armed reconnaissance across the Potomac (*pages 166-167*). Stuart's three-day ride took him into Maryland and Pennsylvania and then back to Virginia. It was the second time since June that Stuart had led Confederate cavalry all the way around McClellan's army, and Lincoln was infuriated.

The day after Stuart and his men galloped back into Virginia, Lincoln wrote McClellan a long letter of pointed advice. It was based on an elementary maxim of geometry. The enemy army, by nature of its position in the Shenandoah Valley west of the Blue Ridge, would have to take a roundabout route south and east through the mountain passes in order to defend the Confederate capital of Richmond. But McClellan could take what Lincoln called the "inside track," which lay east of the Blue Ridge, and march directly upon Richmond. Lee's route, wrote Lincoln, "is the arc of a circle, while yours is the chord." McClellan could beat Lee to Richmond or intercept him en route — "unless you admit that he is more than your equal on a march."

While McClellan mulled over the advice, Lincoln decided to draw a limit on his own forbearance. Fearing that McClellan was "playing false — that he did not want to hurt the enemy," Lincoln privately set a test for his general. "I saw how he could intercept the enemy on the way to Richmond," the President later explained to his private secretary John Hay. "If he let them get away I would remove him."

On October 26, nearly six weeks after the Battle of Antietam, McClellan finally set his army — reinforced to 110,000 men — in motion. His vanguard crossed the Potomac

A Wild Sweep by Confederate Horsemen

J.W. RANDOLPH RICHMOND V^A
LITH BY E CREHEN

The sheet-music cover of "Riding a Raid," a popular song written after Stuart's first ride around the Army of the Potomac in June 1862, features the dashing cavalry chief on a powerful warhorse. After Stuart's Chambersburg raid, the song became doubly popular.

On October 9, 1862, Major General Jeb Stuart and 1,800 Confederate cavalrymen launched a daring raid into Maryland and Pennsylvania that netted them considerable booty and caused the Federals grave embarrassment. Stuart's objectives were to gain information about the Army of the Potomac and to destroy the railroad bridge at Chambersburg, Pennsylvania, over which half the supplies for the army passed.

At dawn on October 10, the raiders crossed the Potomac and headed north into Maryland, arresting travelers who might report their presence — except the women they encountered, whom Stuart gallantly allowed to proceed on their way. At dusk, the Confederates reached Chambersburg. The town was undefended, but the iron railroad bridge defied destruction. Realizing that the Federals would soon be on their trail, Stuart ordered the supply depot burned — but not before his men had helped themselves to the contents.

Now a desperate race to the Potomac began. Stuart rode east toward Gettysburg, then turned south, reentering Maryland above Emmitsburg. From a captured Federal he learned that his pursuers were waiting for him at Frederick, 20 miles ahead. Traveling on back roads, he slipped between two forces of Federal troops to recross the Potomac south of Frederick early on October 12. He brought with him 1,200 captured horses, 30 local officials who could be exchanged for Confederate civil prisoners, and valuable intelligence about Federal troop locations. In three days his troopers had traveled 126 miles — at a cost of only one man wounded and two missing.

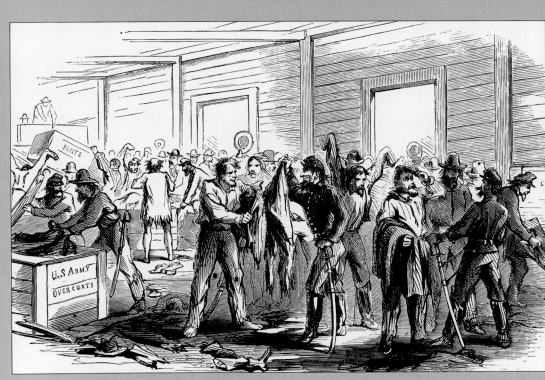

Stuart's raiders rummage through crates of new U.S. Army clothing at the Federal supply depot in Chambersburg, Pennsylvania. Many of the Confederates prized the blue overcoats and wore them on the way back to Virginia, causing some Federals to mistake the riders for friendly troops.

A cooperative civilian gives directions to a Confederate officer as Stuart's men approach Barnesville, Maryland, on their ride back to Virginia. Under observation by the Federal signal station on Sugar Loaf Mountain (*background*), Stuart eluded the Federals by turning into the wooded area south of Barnesville.

over a new pontoon bridge at Berlin, five miles downstream from Harpers Ferry. Following Lincoln's suggested "inside track," the troops then marched south toward Warrenton, Virginia, where McClellan intended to concentrate his forces before pushing on.

Lee, meanwhile, moved to thwart the Federal advance by once again dividing his army. On October 28, he left Stonewall Jackson in the Shenandoah Valley and took half the army on a swift, 60-mile march south and east through the passes of the Blue Ridge. By the time the Federal vanguard reached the vicinity of Warrenton, Lee had established himself at Culpeper Court House, 20 miles to the southwest. From this position he could oppose a Federal march on Richmond.

To Lincoln this meant that the enemy had gotten away again. McClellan had failed his test. Lincoln confided to his old friend and trusted adviser, Francis Preston Blair, that he "had tried long enough to bore with an auger too dull to take hold. He has got the slows, Mr. Blair."

There was more to it. Lincoln had indulged McClellan's "slows" before, but times had changed. As a conservative Democrat, McClellan stood for limited war and compromise. Lincoln's Emancipation Proclamation had doomed all possibility of meeting the Confederacy halfway. For the North, the War was now being waged not only to preserve the Union but to abolish slavery. McClellan, with his overwhelming caution and his reluctance to sacrifice the lives of his soldiers, did not possess the ardor to fight such an all-out war.

This then was one last and ironic consequence of the Union's strategic success at Antietam: Its author must go.

On November 5, the President had orders drawn up relieving McClellan of command of the Army of the Potomac and replacing him with General Burnside. Secretary of War Stanton was so worried that McClellan might refuse to step down, or that the army might mutiny, that he arranged extraordinary procedures for delivering the orders. He entrusted them to his high-ranking assistant, Brigadier General Catharinus P. Buckingham, and instructed him to take a special train to the army's field headquarters north of Warrenton.

Buckingham arrived at his first stop, Burnside's headquarters near Salem, late on November 7 in the midst of an unseasonably early snowstorm. Burnside, as he had on two previous occasions, refused to accept command of the army, protesting that he was not qualified. But when Buckingham, acting under Stanton's instructions, informed him that the command would go to Hooker, his bitter rival, if he did not accept it, Burnside relented.

Buckingham and Burnside then boarded the train together and rode a few miles up the line to Rectortown. It was about 11 p.m. and McClellan was writing a letter to his wife when the two generals appeared at the entrance to his tent.

McClellan received them cordially. He had girded himself for this moment; he had heard about the special train and he expected to be sacked. The shock came with the news of his successor: his old friend Burnside, whom he now regarded as "not fit to command more than a regiment."

McClellan carefully concealed his emotions as he read the orders. "I am sure that not the slightest expression of feeling was visible on my face," McClellan wrote his

In the sketch, handwritten annotations read:
"Berlin" ... "Burnside's Corps" ... "on Thursday Oct 27th over the pontoon bridge into Virginia, at the town of" ... "1862" ... "E.F." ... "I cannot finish this the mail goes" ... "immediately"

At Berlin, Maryland, on October 27, 1862, troops of General Burnside's IX Corps, pursuing Lee's army, file down the C & O Canal towpath and cross a pontoon bridge to the Virginia shore of the Potomac. When artist Edwin Forbes drew this sketch for *Leslie's Illustrated Weekly,* he used numerals to locate key landmarks for his editors.

wife later that night. "They have made a great mistake. Alas for my poor country! I know in my inmost heart she never had a truer servant."

McClellan was instructed to return immediately to his home in Trenton, New Jersey, where he was to await "further orders" — orders that would never come. In response to Burnside's pleas, however, he agreed to remain for a few days to help with the transition in command.

McClellan would also get an opportunity to say good-by to his troops — for him a most reluctant farewell. "The Army of the Potomac is my army as much as any army ever belonged to the man that created it," he had remarked to one of his aides only three weeks before. "We are wedded and should not be separated."

Most of the men felt the same way. Brigadier General John Gibbon described the army as *"Thunderstruck.* There is but one opinion among the troops and that is that the government has gone mad." Lieutenant Edgar Newcomb of the 19th Massachusetts concurred. "If McClellan wished to establish himself Supreme Dictator today," he wrote, "the army in the heat of their resentment of this wrong would be with him."

When McClellan reviewed his troops for the last time on November 10, there were scenes of great emotion. In a flamboyant gesture of affection and protest, color-bearers of the Irish Brigade flung down their banners in his path. Soldiers wept, muttered about marching on Washington and called out in his wake, "Send him back! Send him back!" Some of the men broke ranks and gathered around McClellan as he rode past them. Others, wrote Colonel Charles Wainwright, "could be seen gazing after him in mute grief, one may almost say despair, as a mourner looks down into the grave of a dearly loved friend."

On the following day, McClellan boarded his train at Warrenton Junction. The general stepped out onto the rear platform of his car and calmed the distraught men of his honor guard with a little speech. "Stand by General Burnside as you have stood by me," he urged them, "and all will be well. Good-by lads."

Then the train steamed slowly out of the station carrying Little Mac away from the War for the last time. "A shade of sadness crossed his face," noted Colonel Edward Cross of the 5th New Hampshire. "He carried the hearts of the army with him."

Doffing his kepi, General McClellan bids farewell to the Army of the Potomac near Warrenton, Virginia, on November 10, 1862. Riding alongside McClellan is his successor, Major General Ambrose E. Burnside.

ACKNOWLEDGMENTS

The editors wish to thank the following individuals and institutions for their valuable assistance in the preparation of this volume:
Connecticut: New Milford — Norm Flayderman.
Delaware: Wilmington — Scott Harrington.
Maryland: Annapolis — Nancy Bramucci, Maryland Hall of Records. Clinton — Bill Turner. Sharpsburg — Betty Otto, Antietam National Battlefield.
New York: Delhi — Herbert Sorgen, State University of New York Agricultural and Technical College. Oneonta — James Milne Library, State University of New York.
Pennsylvania: Carlisle — Randy Hackenburg, Michael J. Winey, U.S. Army Military History Institute.
Vermont: Middlebury — John M. McCardell Jr.
Virginia: Richmond — David Hahn, Museum of the Confederacy; Virginius Hall, Rebecca Perrine, Virginia Historical Society.
Washington, D.C.: Carol Johnson, Eveline Nave, Bernard Riley, Library of Congress.
West Virginia: Harpers Ferry — Dennis Frye, Hilda E. Staubs, Harpers Ferry National Historical Park.
The following source was particularly valuable in the preparation of this volume: *Landscape Turned Red: The Battle of Antietam,* by Stephen W. Sears, Ticknor & Fields, 1983.

The index for this book was prepared by Nicholas J. Anthony.

PICTURE CREDITS

The sources for the illustrations in this book are shown below. Credits from left to right are separated by semicolons, from top to bottom by dashes.

COVER: John L. McGuire Collection, courtesy William A. Frassanito. 2, 3: Map by Peter McGinn. 9: Painting attributed to W. B. Cox, courtesy The Virginia Historical Society, Richmond, Virginia. 10: Maryland State Archives, photographed by Henry Beville. 11: Virginia Historical Society, Richmond, Virginia. 12: Sketch by Alfred R. Waud, Library of Congress. 14: National Archives Civil War Neg. No. 168. 16: Courtesy Antietam National Battlefield, Sharpsburg, Maryland, photographed by Larry Sherer. 18, 19: Courtesy Mrs. Benjamin Rosenstock. 20: Courtesy Frank & Marie-T. Wood Print Collections, Alexandria, Virginia. 22: Map by Walter W. Roberts. 24, 25: Inset, Valentine Museum, Richmond, Virginia; Museum of the Confederacy, Richmond, Virginia, photographed by Larry Sherer. 26, 27: Courtesy Frank & Marie-T. Wood Print Collections, Alexandria, Virginia. 28, 29: Drawing by Edwin Forbes, Library of Congress. 30, 31: National Park Service; National Archives Neg. No. 79-CWC-3F-26. 32, 33: Special Collections, U.S. Military Academy Library, copied by Henry Groskinsky; courtesy The New-York Historical Society, New York City. 34, 35: Library of Congress. 36, 37: National Park Service. 39: Virginia Military Institute Museum, Lexington, Virginia, photographed by Larry Sherer. 40, 41: Painting by William MacLeod: *Maryland Heights: Siege of Harper's Ferry,* The Corcoran Gallery of Art, gift of Genevieve Plummer. 42: Courtesy Lightfoot Collection. 46, 47: Library of Congress. 48: Map by Walter W. Roberts. 50: Military Order of the Loyal Legion of the United States-Massachusetts/U.S. Army Military History Institute (MOLLUS-Mass./USAMHI), copied by Peter Ralston. 51: Library of Congress — courtesy Bill Turner. 52, 53: Courtesy Frank & Marie-T. Wood Print Collections, Alexandria, Virginia. 54: *Civil War Times Illustrated.* 55: From *War Talks of Confederate Veterans,* © 1892 by George S. Bernard, published 1981 by Morningside House, Inc., Dayton, Ohio. 56: State Historical Society of Wisconsin Neg. No. WHi(X3)40390. 58: Division of Military and Naval Affairs, State of New York, photographed by Henry Groskinsky. 61: Courtesy Frank & Marie-T. Wood Print Collections, Alexandria, Virginia. 62, 63: Library of Congress. 65: Painting by Lachlan Field, courtesy Joseph Whitehorne, photographed by Henry Beville. 66, 67: Drawing by Alfred R. Waud, Library of Congress. 68: Painting by L. E. Faber, West Point Museum Collections, U.S. Military Academy, photographed by Henry Groskinsky. 69: Map by Walter W. Roberts. 71: Library of Congress. 72, 73: American Heritage Picture Collection. 74: National Archives Neg. No. 111-B-4091. 75: MOLLUS-Mass./USAMHI, copied by Peter Ralston. 76, 77: Inset from *Battles and Leaders of the Civil War,* Vol. 2, published by The Century Co., New York, 1887 — Library of Congress. 78: Map by Walter W. Roberts. 79: Museum of the Confederacy, Richmond, Virginia. 80, 81: Courtesy Frank & Marie-T. Wood Print Collections, Alexandria, Virginia. 82: National Archives Neg. No. 111-BA-61. 84, 85: Painting by Thure de Thulstrup, courtesy Seventh Regiment Fund, Inc., photographed by Al Freni. 87: Courtesy Michael J. McAfee. 88: Drawing by Alfred R. Waud, Library of Congress. 89: Courtesy Daniel Miller, copied by Nemo Warr. 90: Courtesy Bill Turner, copied by Steve Tuttle. 92: MOLLUS-Mass./USAMHI, copied by Peter Ralston. 93: *Civil War Times Illustrated.* 94, 95: Library of Congress. 96: MOLLUS-Mass./USAMHI, photographed by Peter Ralston. 97: Drawing by Alfred R. Waud, Library of Congress. 98: Map by Walter W. Roberts. 99: From *Battles and Leaders of the Civil War,* Vol. 2, published by The Century Co., New York, 1887. 101: Division of Military and Naval Affairs, State of New York, photographed by Henry Groskinsky. 102: From *Battles and Leaders of the Civil War,* Vol. 2, published by The Century Co., New York, 1887. 104: Drawing attributed to Arthur Lumley, Library of Congress. 106: National Archives Civil War Neg. No. 140 — Valentine Museum, Richmond, Virginia; Library of Congress; MOLLUS-Mass./USAMHI, copied by Peter Ralston (2). 107: Library of Congress (3); U.S. Army Military History Institute, copied by Peter Ralston — courtesy Michael J. McAfee. 109: Drawing by Alfred R. Waud, Library of Congress. 110-117: Paintings by James Hope, courtesy Antietam National Battlefield, Sharpsburg, Maryland, photographed by Larry Sherer. 118, 119: Painting by James Hope, courtesy The Kennedy Galleries, New York City, photographed by Henry Groskinsky. 121: Courtesy Daniel Miller, copied by Nemo Warr. 122: Courtesy Brian Pohanka. 123: Library of Congress. 124: Meserve Collection, National Portrait Gallery, Smithsonian Institution, Washington, D.C. 125: National Archives Neg. No. 111-B-5808. 126: Courtesy Harry Roach. 127: Division of Military and Naval Affairs, State of New York, photographed by Henry Groskinsky — courtesy Michael J. McAfee. 128, 129: Drawing by Edwin Forbes, Library of Congress. 130: Map by Walter W. Roberts. 131: Old Court House Museum, Vicksburg, Mississippi. 132: Drawing by Edwin Forbes, Library of Congress. 133: White, Wellford, Taliaferro and Marshall Family Papers (#1300), Southern Historical Collection, Library of the University of North Carolina at Chapel Hill. 134, 135: Library of Congress; courtesy Frank & Marie-T. Wood Print Collections, Alexandria, Virginia. 136: National Archives Neg. No. 111-B-1857. 138-147: Library of Congress. 148: John L. McGuire Collection, courtesy William A. Frassanito. 149: MOLLUS-Mass./USAMHI, courtesy William A. Frassanito. 151: Courtesy Norm Flayderman, photographed by Henry Groskinsky. 152: Drawing by Alfred R. Waud, Library of Congress. 154, 155: Courtesy Frank & Marie-T. Wood Print Collections, Alexandria, Virginia. 157: The Western Reserve Historical Society, Cleveland, Ohio. 158, 159: Library of Congress. 160: Print Room, The New York Public Library, Astor, Lenox and Tilden Foundations. 162-165: Library of Congress, courtesy James R. Mellon. 166: The South Caroliniana Library, University of South Carolina. 167: Courtesy Frank & Marie-T. Wood Print Collections, Alexandria, Virginia. 169: Drawing by Edwin Forbes, Library of Congress. 170, 171: Drawing by Alfred R. Waud, Library of Congress.

BIBLIOGRAPHY

Books

Alexander, E. P., *Military Memoirs of a Confederate: A Critical Narrative.* Press of Morningside Bookshop, 1977.
Allan, William, *The Army of Northern Virginia in 1862.* Houghton, Mifflin and Company, 1892.
Andrews, J. Cutler, *The South Reports the Civil War.* Princeton University Press, 1970.
Bates, Samuel P., *Martial Deeds of Pennsylvania.* T. H. Davis & Co., 1876.
Bernard, Geo. S., ed., *War Talks of Confederate Veterans.* Press of Morningside Bookshop, 1981.
Beyer, W. F., and O. F. Keydel, eds., *Deeds of Valor from Records in the Archives of the United States Government.* The Perrien-Keydel Company, 1906.
Blackford, W. W., *War Years with Jeb Stuart.* Charles Scribner's Sons, 1945.
Borcke, Heros von, *Memoirs of the Confederate War for Independence.* J. B. Lippincott & Co., 1867.
Bridges, Hal, *Lee's Maverick General: Daniel Harvey Hill.* McGraw-Hill Book Company, Inc., 1961.
Bruce, George A., *The Twentieth Regiment of Massachusetts Volunteer Infantry, 1861-1865.* Houghton, Mifflin and Company, 1906.
Bruce, Robert V., *Lincoln and the Tools of War.* The Bobbs-Merrill Company, Inc., 1956.
Carter, Robert Goldthwaite, *Four Brothers in Blue, or Sunshine and Shadows of the War of the Rebellion.* University of Texas Press, 1978.
Casler, John O., *Four Years in the Stonewall Brigade.* Press of Morningside Bookshop, 1981.
Catton, Bruce:
Mr. Lincoln's Army. Doubleday & Company, Inc., 1951.
Terrible Swift Sword (The Centennial History of the Civil War, Vol. 2). Pocket Books, 1963.
Child, William, *A History of the Fifth Regiment New Hampshire Volunteers.* R. W. Musgrove, Printer, 1893.

Commager, Henry Steele, ed., *The Blue and the Gray: The Story of the Civil War as Told by Participants*, Vol. 2. The Bobbs-Merrill Company, 1973.

Congdon, Don, ed., *Combat: The Civil War*. Delacorte Press, 1967.

Cox, Jacob D., *Military Reminiscences of the Civil War*, Vol. 1. Charles Scribner's Sons, 1900.

Davenport, Alfred, *Camp and Field Life of the Fifth New York Volunteer Infantry*. Dick and Fitzgerald, 1879.

Davis, Charles E., Jr., *Three Years in the Army: The Story of the Thirteenth Massachusetts Volunteers*. Estes and Lauriat, 1894.

Douglas, Henry Kyd, *I Rode with Stonewall*. Mockingbird Books, Inc., 1979.

Dowdey, Clifford, *Lee*. Little, Brown and Company, 1965.

Dwight, Wilder, *Life and Letters of Wilder Dwight*. Ticknor and Fields, 1868.

Dyer, John P., *The Gallant Hood*. The Bobbs-Merrill Company, 1950.

Early, Jubal Anderson, *Lieutenant General Jubal Anderson Early, C.S.A.: Autobiographical Sketch and Narrative of the War between the States*. J. B. Lippincott Company, 1912.

Fox, William F., *Regimental Losses in the American Civil War, 1861-1865*. Albany Publishing Company, 1889.

Frassanito, William A., *Antietam: The Photographic Legacy of America's Bloodiest Day*. Charles Scribner's Sons, 1978.

Freeman, Douglas Southall:
Lee's Lieutenants: A Study in Command, Vol. 2. Charles Scribner's Sons, 1943.
R. E. Lee: A Biography, Vol. 2. Charles Scribner's Sons, 1934.

Freeman, Larry, *The Hope Paintings*. Century House, 1961.

Gibbon, John, *Personal Recollections of the Civil War*. Press of Morningside Bookshop, 1978.

Glover, Edwin A., *Bucktailed Wildcats*. Thomas Yoseloff, 1960.

Gould, John M., *History of the First-Tenth-Twenty-ninth Maine Regiment*. Stephen Berry, 1871.

Hall, Isaac, *History of the Ninety-seventh Regiment New York Volunteers*. Press of L. C. Childs & Son, 1890.

Harwell, Richard B., *The Union Reader*. Longmans, Green and Co., 1958.

Hassler, Warren W., Jr., *General George B. McClellan: Shield of the Union*. Louisiana State University Press, 1957.

Hassler, William Woods, *A. P. Hill: Lee's Forgotten General*. The University of North Carolina Press, 1962.

Henderson, G.F.R., *Stonewall Jackson and the American Civil War*, Vol. 2. Longmans, Green, and Co., 1909.

Hitchcock, Frederick L., *War from the Inside: The Story of the 132nd Regiment Pennsylvania Volunteer Infantry in the War for the Suppression of the Rebellion*. Press of J. B. Lippincott Company, 1904.

Hood, J. B., *Advance and Retreat*. G. T. Beauregard, 1880.

Johnson, Robert Underwood, and Clarence Clough Buel, eds., *Battles and Leaders of the Civil War*, Vols. 2 and 3. Thomas Yoseloff, Inc., 1956.

Lee, Robert E., *The Wartime Papers of R. E. Lee*. Ed. by Clifford Dowdey. Bramhall House, 1961.

Leech, Margaret, *Reveille in Washington, 1860-1865*. Time-Life Books, 1980.

Lindeman, Jack, ed., *The Conflict of Convictions*. Chilton Book Company, 1968.

Longstreet, James, *From Manassas to Appomattox*. Ed. by James I. Robertson Jr. Indiana University Press, 1960.

McClellan, George B.:

McClellan's Own Story: The War for the Union. Charles L. Webster & Company, 1887.
Report on the Organization and Campaigns of the Army of the Potomac. Sheldon & Company, 1864.

Michie, Peter S., *General McClellan*. D. Appleton and Company, 1915.

Military Historical Society of Massachusetts, *Campaigns in Virginia, Maryland and Pennsylvania, 1862-1863*. Griffith-Stillings Press, 1903.

Mills, Charles J., *Through Blood and Fire: The Civil War Letters of Major Charles J. Mills*. Ed. by Gregory A. Coco. Gregory A. Coco, 1982.

Murfin, James V., *The Gleam of Bayonets: The Battle of Antietam and the Maryland Campaign of 1862*. Louisiana State University Press, 1965.

Nevins, Allan, *War Becomes Revolution, 1862-1863 (The War for the Union*, Vol. 2). Charles Scribner's Sons, 1960.

Nolan, Alan T., *The Iron Brigade*. The Macmillan Company, 1961.

Noyes, George F., *The Bivouac and the Battle-field; or, Campaign Sketches in Virginia and Maryland*. Harper & Brothers, 1863.

Oates, Stephen B., *With Malice toward None: The Life of Abraham Lincoln*. Harper & Row, 1977.

Palfrey, Francis Winthrop, *The Antietam and Fredericksburg (Campaigns of the Civil War*, Vol. 5). Charles Scribner's Sons, 1882.

Pettengill, S. B., *The College Cavaliers*. H. McAllaster & Co., Printers, 1883.

Pullen, John J., *The Twentieth Maine: A Volunteer Regiment in the Civil War*. Press of Morningside Bookshop, 1980.

Sandburg, Carl, *Abraham Lincoln: The War Years*, Vol. 1. Harcourt, Brace & Company, 1939.

Sanford, George B., *Fighting Rebels and Redskins: Experiences in Army Life of Colonel George B. Sanford, 1861-1892*. Ed. by E. R. Hagemann. University of Oklahoma Press, 1969.

Schenck, Martin, *Up Came Hill: The Story of the Light Division and Its Leaders*. The Stackpole Company, 1958.

Schildt, John W.:
Drums along the Antietam. McClain Printing Company, 1972.
Four Days in October. John W. Schildt, 1978.
September Echoes: The Maryland Campaign of 1862. The Valley Register, 1960.

Simons, Ezra D., *A Regimental History: The One Hundred and Twenty-fifth New York State Volunteers*. Ezra D. Simons, 1888.

Simpson, Harold B., *Hood's Texas Brigade: Lee's Grenadier Guard*. Alcor Publishing Company, 1983.

Stackpole, Edward J., *From Cedar Mountain to Antietam: August-September, 1862*. The Stackpole Company, 1959.

Starr, Louis M., *Bohemian Brigade: Civil War Newsmen in Action*. Alfred A. Knopf, 1954.

Strong, George Templeton, *Diary of the Civil War, 1860-1865*. Ed. by Allan Nevins. The Macmillan Company, 1962.

Strother, David Hunter, *A Virginia Yankee in the Civil War: The Diaries of David Hunter Strother*. Ed. by Cecil D. Eby Jr. The University of North Carolina Press, 1961.

Survivors' Association, 118th Pennsylvania Infantry, *History of the 118th Pennsylvania Volunteers: Corn Exchange Regiment*. J. L. Smith, 1905.

Swinton, William, *Campaigns of the Army of the Potomac*. Charles Scribner's Sons, 1882.

Teetor, Paul R., *A Matter of Hours: Treason at Harper's Ferry*. Fairleigh Dickinson University Press, 1982.

Thomas, Benjamin P., *Abraham Lincoln*. Alfred A. Knopf, 1952.

Thomas, Benjamin P., and Harold M. Hyman, *Stanton*. Alfred A. Knopf, 1962.

Thomas, Howard, *Boys in Blue from the Adirondack Foothills*. Prospect Books, 1960.

Todd, William, ed., *History of the Ninth Regiment, N.Y.S.M., N.G.S.N.Y. (Eighty-third New York Volunteers)*. Veterans of the Ninth Regiment, 1889.

United States War Department, *The War of the Rebellion: A Compilation of the Official Records of the Union and Confederate Armies*, Series I, Vol. 19. Government Printing Office, 1887.

Vandiver, Frank E., *Mighty Stonewall*. McGraw-Hill Book Company, Inc., 1957.

Wainwright, Charles S., *A Diary of Battle: The Personal Journals of Colonel Charles S. Wainwright, 1861-1865*. Ed. by Allan Nevins. Harcourt, Brace & World, Inc., 1962.

Walcott, Charles F., *History of the Twenty-first Regiment Massachusetts Volunteers*. Houghton, Mifflin and Company, 1882.

Walker, Francis A., *History of the Second Army Corps in the Army of the Potomac*. Charles Scribner's Sons, 1886.

Welles, Gideon, *Diary of Gideon Welles*, Vol. 1. Houghton Mifflin Company, 1911.

Wiley, Bell Irvin, *The Life of Billy Yank: The Common Soldier of the Union*. Louisiana State University Press, 1981.

Williams, Alpheus S., *From the Cannon's Mouth: The Civil War Letters of General Alpheus S. Williams*. Ed. by Milo M. Quaife. Wayne State University Press and the Detroit Historical Society, 1959.

Williams, Kenneth P., *Lincoln Finds a General: A Military Study of the Civil War*, Vol. 1. The Macmillan Company, 1949.

Williams, T. Harry:
Hayes of the Twenty-third. Alfred A. Knopf, 1965.
Lincoln and His Generals. Alfred A. Knopf, 1952.
Lincoln and the Radicals. The University of Wisconsin Press, 1941.

Willson, Arabella M., *Disaster, Struggle, Triumph*. The Argus Company, 1870.

Wise, Jennings Cropper, *The Long Arm of Lee: The History of the Artillery of the Army of Northern Virginia*. Oxford University Press, 1959.

Wistar, Isaac Jones, *Autobiography of Isaac Jones Wistar*. The Wistar Institute of Anatomy and Biology, 1937.

Other Sources

"The Battlefield of Antietam." Oliver T. Reilly, 1906.

Kelly, Dennis P., "The Battle of Shepherdstown." *Civil War Times Illustrated*, November 1981.

Luff, William M., "March of the Cavalry from Harper's Ferry, September 14, 1862." *Military Essays and Recollections: Papers Read before the Commandery of the State of Illinois, Military Order of the Loyal Legion of the United States*, Vol. 2. A. C. McClurg and Company, 1894.

Ripley, Edward H., "Memories of the Ninth Vermont at the Tragedy of Harper's Ferry, Sept. 15, 1862." *Personal Recollections of the War of the Rebellion: Addresses Delivered before the Commandery of the State of New York, Military Order of the Loyal Legion of the United States*. Ed. by A. Noel Blakeman. G. P. Putnam's Sons, 1912.

Strother, David Hunter, "Personal Recollections of the War by a Virginian." *Harper's New Monthly Magazine*, February 1868.

INDEX